A YEAR OF POETRY TEA TIME

POETRY IN WINTER

Teacher Resource with Over 100 Poems, Vocabulary, Hands-on Activities, and Poetry Writing Lessons

Also by Christine Owens
Relaxed Homeschooling
A Year of Poetry Tea Time
A Year of Poetry Tea Time Patriotism
A Year of Poetry Tea Time Adventure
A Year of Poetry Tea Time Journals
My 50 Book Reading Journals

A YEAR OF POETRY TEA TIME

POETRY IN WINTER

Written and Edited by

Christine Owens

To download your FREE Vocabulary Flashcards

Visit **www.AYearofPoetryTeaTime.com/shop**

And use the code "WINTER" at checkout

Poetry In Winter: Teacher Resource with Over 100 Poems, Vocabulary, Hands-on Activities, and Poetry Writing Lessons

Copyright © 2020 Christine Owens
Published by Whimsy Rock Press
All rights reserved.
No original material of this publication may be reproduced, distributed, or transmitted in any form or by any means, including photocopying, recording or other electronic or mechanical method, without the written permission of the publisher, except in the case of brief quotations embodied in reviews, articles, and certain other non-commercial uses permitted by copyright law.
Any mention in this book pertaining to my experiences are purely that, my experiences, and should not be taken as legal advice when navigating your in-home educational choices. Each household must do what is best for their own family, classroom, or homeschool.

First Printing, 2023

Sketched Illustrations by Quentin Owens
Cover Designed by Christine Owens

Owens, Christine
Poetry In Winter: Teacher Resource with Over 100 Poems, Vocabulary, Hands-on Activities, and Poetry Writing Lessons
ISBN: 978-1-954270-26-8
ISBN: 978-1-954270-27-5 (electronic)

Sketched Illustrations by Quentin Owens

Cover designed by Christine Owens

**This book is dedicated to
My Great Aunt Lou and "Aunt" Jean
for so many fond Christmas memories**

Acknowledgments

Thank you to the following people and their businesses for judging and promoting the 2023 International Homeschool Poetry contest

Platinum Sponsor

Tuttle Twins Cartoon
www.Angel.com/tuttleIG
A cartoon where a grandma with a time-traveling wheelchair takes her twin grandkids on hilarious adventures to learn
about freedom and economics.

Judges

Andrew Pudewa
www.iew.com
The Institute for Excellence in Writing

Michelle Heidenrich Barnes
www.michellehbarnes.com
Published Poet/author

Matt Forrest Esenwine
www.mattforrest.com
published poet/author

Aimee Lucido
chttp://www.aimeelucido.com/
Published poet/author

Greg Denning
www.worldschoolacademy.com
Life coach for men, marriage, homeschooling mentor, and owner of World School Academy

Amanda Schenkenberger
www.Moms.heartsmarthomeschool.com
Homeschool anxiety free with

Sarah Janisse Brown
www.funschooling.com
Funschooling is fun for kids, effective at helping them learn, and easy for moms.

Donna Goff
www.mentoringourown.com
Bring life to your homeschool, inspire your children to love learning, and thrive!

Table of Contents

Introduction *17*
How to Use the book *19*
Discussing Poetry with Children *22*
Poetry Styles & Terms *28*
December *33*
Winter *34*
    Storm 34
    Winter 34
    Mistress Winter 35
    Approach of Winter 35
    A Tree In Winter 36
    Winter 37
    Winter Moon 37
    Winter Voice 38
    Spellbound 39
    Jack Frost 40
        Koch Fractal Snowflake Activity 41
Hanukkah *44*
    The Power of Brotherhood & Faith 44
    Chanukah Dreams 45
    Miracles 46
        Traditional Sufganiyot Cooking Activity 47
        Nana Tea Making Activity 49
    Legendary Lights 50
Children in Winter *51*
    What Is Winter? 51
    Three Little Kittens 52
    A Wish Of When 53
    Sneezles 54

Smiling Girls, Rosy Boys	56
Saint Nicholas	56

Winter Treats 57

Sticky Licking Peppermint	57
Peppermint Ornaments Craft Activity	58
Peppermint Pillows Cooking Activity	58
When Good King Arthur Ruled The Land	60
Handy Spandy Jack-a-Dandy	60
Catching Chocolate	60
Home Made Hot Cocoa Cooking Activity	61
Polly Put The Kettle On	62
Little Jack Horner	62

Christmas 63

The Christmas Tree	63
Like A Twinkling Tannenbaum	64
Across Delaware	64
Snow and Snow	64
Gifts At Christmas	64
Haiku Fun Poetry Writing Activity	65
The Christmas Wreath	66
Dark Night Caroling	67
Christmas	68
Christmas Bells	69

Religious Christmas 71

Christmastide	71
Carol Of The Russian Children	71
December 25, 1914	72
Cradle Hymn	74
Carol	74
The Three Kings	75

December Poetry Writing Prompts 78

December Vocabulary Cards 79

January 86

    The Months 87

The New Year 88

    New Year's Colors 88

    I Saw Three Ships 90

    Resolution 90

        Shape Poetry Writing Activity 91

    Haiku On Goals 98

    May His Life Have Had Purpose 98

Winter Fun 99

    If It Were January All The Year 99

    Down We Go 99

    Snowball 100

    Snowball Fight 100

        Making Snow Tactile Activity 101

        Indoor Snowball Fight P.E. Activity 101

    Wanderlust 103

    The Sugar-Plum Tree 104

        Gingerbread Loaf Cooking Activity 105

    Sounds of Their Feet 107

    Snow 108

    The Wassail Song 108

        Wassail Cooking Activity 109

Sleigh Bells 110

    The Bells 110

    Sleigh-Bells 111

    Jingle Bells 112

    Repeat Stanza Two 113

    I'm January 113

Warm Fire 114

    When My Fire Burns Low 114

    A Snowman 114

    The Southern Cross Hearth 114

    I Shiver So Cold 116

    My Fire Pit 116

    Jack Be Nimble 116

Cold of Snow **117**

    Stopping By Woods On A Snowy Evening 117

    Snow Notes 117

    Winter 118

    Winter-Time 118

    Winter Grandeur 120

    Winter's Requiem 121

January Poetry Writing Prompts **123**

January Vocabulary Cards **124**

February **131**

Winter Sleep **132**

    Hush, Baby, My Dolly, I Pray You Don't Cry 132

    The Sleepy Song 132

    Late 133

    Cradle Song 134

    A Cup Of Tea 135

        Cambric Tea Making Activity 136

LOVE **138**

    My Loves 138

    If Love Were Mine 138

    Valentine's Day 139

    Cupid's Arrow 139

    A Red, Red Rose 140

        Love Bath Bombs Science Activity 141

Presidents 144
A Little Boy and a Cherry Tree 144
Washington 144
Washington's Birthday..144
My Childhood Home I See Again 145
The People, Yes..147
This Dust was Once the Man 148

Snowy Mountain 149
Fresh Snow 149
Blizzard Hike 149
The Peak 150
Yeti 150
A Winter's Tale 152
An Arrogant Journey Of A River 152
Winter Trees 153
Sledding...153
Acrostic Poetry Writing Activity 154

Winter Animals 156
Sing, Little Bird..156
Pine Warbler Thanks 157
Groundhog...157
Shelter 158
Penguins 158
Winter Wolf 159

Chinese New Year 160
Chinese New Year 160
What Will The New Year Bring 160
Poem On Selling Silliness..161
New Years Eve 161
Stay Up Late On New Years Eve..162

New Years Day	163
Snow on New Year's Eve	163
Chinese Almond Cookies Cooking Activity	164

Winters End *166*
Frost	166
My Souls Winter	167
An English Winter	168
The Fairies' Nook in Winter	169

February Poetry Writing Prompts *171*

February Vocabulary Cards *172*

Mini Poet Biographies *179*

BONUS POEMS *203*
Noel: Christmas Eve 1913	203
On the Morning of Christ's Nativity	204

Introduction

Poetry In Winter is designed to make poetry an enjoyable and enlightening experience for both teacher and student. It will help you, whether you are a classroom teacher or homeschooling parent, introduce classic and modern poetry to your students. This is the first book in a series of four with each book focused on a single season. With *Poetry In Winter* you will find a rich collection of poems that will not only explore the winter season but shine a light on other winter topics such as love, presidents, Chinese New Year, childhood fun, and more. It will also help you teach your students how to write 3 different forms of poetry and provide you with vocabulary flashcards and wonderful treats, drinks, and hands-on activities to bring the poems to life.

I promise you that if you use this book for your winter semester/season, you will have fresh new poetry and activities all winter long that will expand your student's vocabulary and increase their literary and emotional understanding.

Inside this book you will find

—The definition of 71 challenging words right under the poem for quick reference
—100+ poems; enough to read one poem every day of the winter months.
—36 printable vocabulary flash cards (12 per month) and blank flash cards to customize your learning experience
—70+ mini poet biographies stuffed full of facts
—12 quotes to promote kindness
—5 hands-on cross-curricular activities; 1 math, 1 science, 2 crafts, 1 P.E.
—8 recipes: 4 delicious drinks and 4 snacks (all inspired by poems) to share with your students
—3 poetry writing lessons, accessible to all ages, to learn how to write haiku, shape, and acrostic poetry.
—36 poetry writing prompts to inspire your students
—Chapters organized by month and themes for quick relevant poetry

WHY IS THIS BOOK FOR YOU?
Not only will *Poetry in Winter* save you a lot of time, but it will make it a breeze to introduce poetry to your students. With the right exposure, children from ages two to seventeen can learn to appreciate the poetry of A. A. Milne, as well as Longfellow. Don't miss out on the mind-expanding experience of poetry.

This curated collection will be a valuable addition to every classroom and homeschool. It's not going to just sit on your shelf…**it will be right there at arms reach to enrich your learning experience**. There is no planning needed, just "open and go." Not only is the poetry from all over the world, it covers a broad timeline from as 854 BC to present. Not only will they hear the words of some of the world's greatest poets but also be inspired by award winning poetry written by children of all ages.

Through poetry, not only do children start to understand literary concepts, like imagery and rhyme, they also expand their minds by engaging in critical-thinking, problem-solving, and they develop emotional intelligence. So what are you waiting for??? Add excitement and learning to your lesson now with *Poetry in Winter*.

How to Use the book

I created this book to take the stress out of exploring poetry with your class. Spending the time to find relevant and age-appropriate poetry can be very time consuming, especially if your students are young or poetry is new to you. Put your past poetry experience behind you and don't let it scare you away. Poetry is as accessible to you and your students as the songs you hear on the radio every day.

Original punctuation, spelling, and emphasis have been maintained from the original poetic works. Additionally, unique, poem formatting was kept to the original format where possible.

DISCUSSING POETRY WITH CHILDREN
This section provides you with open ended questions you can ask your students about poems you read. They are divided into categories so you have many options to choose from and still be relevant to the poem. For instance, if a poem feels as if it is supposed to evoke emotion then you can choose a question under the "Questions Related to Feeling section.
Tip: Don't be afraid to ask your students a question even if you don't totally understand the poem the first time you read it.

TEACHERS DEEPER UNDERSTANDING
This section will help you better understand the three styles of poetry that have poetry writing lessons connected to them. In this book there are poetry writing lessons on haiku, shape, and acrostic poetry. This section will give you tidbits and facts to share with your students and give yourself a firmer grasp on what this style is about.
TIP: Share the interesting facts with your students and then bring them up throughout the month and see who can remember them.

POETRY STYLES & TERMS
This section will help you learn about different poetry styles and terms. This will help you better educate your students. The three styles that are focused on in this book are in bold for quick reference. A quick read through this section will bring awareness to poetic devices that you run across every day. With this bit of knowledge stored in your back pocked you will be able to point things out to your students on a daily basis.
TIP: Use a sticky note as a bookmark for quick reference.

THE POETRY CHAPTERS
This book was created with the idea that a teacher or parent would be using it as a resource to supplement and enrich their curriculum. For this reason, I have organized the chapters by month. Each month contains poetry that will line up with seasons, holidays, and related themes. Each chapter contains thirty-one or more poems. This gives you a poem to read every single day. Or you could keep it at arm's reach and read a couple poems when you have a few spare moments. This could be just before the bell rings at school, or at home when your children are eating lunch, or when they are tucked into bed.
TIP: *Poems could be assigned for memorization, recitation, or copy work.*

RECIPES
Tucked into each month you will find at least one recipe for a warm drink and baked good. You could either prepare this as a surprise for your students or have a fun cooking activity. Either way, the treats are all delicious and inspired by the poem on the page just before the recipe.
TIP: If you can, let your students be involved in the making process as much as possible.

HANDS-ON ACTIVITIES
In every chapter there is a hands-on activity inspired by a poem on the page before it. Some are very simple, and some will require a little prep, but all of them can be done in both a classroom or at home. Some of these activities have printables included.
TIP: Take a peek at the different activities and plan out which ones you would like to do with your students.

POETRY WRITING ACTIVIY
These poetry writing lessons are found within the separate chapters. The lessons explain how to teach a special poetry style to your students and it will walk you through the steps of how to teach it.
TIP: If you are teaching a group of young children then you can work though the poetry writing with them as a group and create a poem together.

MINI POET BIOGRAPHIES
I have included a mini bio for every single poet featured in this collection. You will find the years they were born and died along with the country they were born in or most popular in. For instance, some poets who became very popular in Australia were actually born in England. When this happens, it is mentioned in their bio where they were actually born. When able, I included what inspired the poet to write poetry and how they received their education. If any poet had a life challenge as a child, I included it so children could see others overcoming obstacles. When possible, I included the ages they were first published, especially if they were published as a child. Often you will find the names of their first publication or their most popular works. When the word "collection" is used, it is referring to a book containing a collection of poetry. A term to keep an eye out for is *posthumous,* which means after the poet's death; some poets had poetry published after they had passed away. Another term used often is *pseudonym* which is another term for pen name.
TIP: Create a poetry timeline and add a poet when you read one of their poems.

QUOTES
Each chapter has four quotes promoting kindness. You can share a new quote every week and hold a short discussion about what the students think it means.
TIP: Print it out and post is someplace for students to see all week.

VOCABULARY FLASH CARDS
Of the 70+ vocabulary words defined in this book, 36 of them were turned into flashcards to make refreshing your new knowledge easier for both teacher and student. There are also blank flashcards for your convenience.
*TIP: Download your **FREE** Vocabulary Flashcards visit www.AYearofPoetryTeaTime.com/shop And use the code "WINTER" at checkout.*

Discussing Poetry with Children

You are about to enter a fun new realm of imagination and intrigue. A world that will have your children laughing, pondering, and looking forward to what they will hear next. Children are capable of having deep conversations and developing critical thinking skills that will shape their future. But remember, all children are different. To some, critical thinking will come naturally, where others need a little help to develop such skills.

Below you will find an array of questions you can ask your children about any poem. Refer to the Poetry Styles & Terms section if you are unfamiliar with any of the poetry vocabulary. The questions are in basic categories to make it easier to find questions that are relevant.

–Make sure to encourage your child to explain their answer. Giving yes or no answers does not show understanding of concepts.

–If your children are at a loss for words, after giving them some silent time to think, then share your thoughts with them and ask if they have any other ideas.

–Don't belittle your child if they don't see or understand a poem, even if it seems obvious to you.

–If you're not sure what a poem means, then give your kids a chance to figure it out.
Poetry is unique as it can mean something to one person and something completely different to another. Remind your children of this concept and embrace their different ideas.

Questions related to poetry terms and style
–Do you think the meaning of this poem is obvious or does it have hidden meanings?
–Does this poem take place in a person's mind (lyric poetry) or at a physical location?
–Does this poem use imagery?
–Does this poem use rhyming words?
–Is this poem a narrative poem, which tells a story?
–Does this poem use satire?
–Did you notice a rhyme scheme in this poem?

–Was this poem meant to be romantic?
–What symbolism was used?

Questions related to feelings
–How did this poem make you feel?
–Do you like how this poem made you feel?
–Have you ever felt this way about something?
–What do you think caused the person to write this poem?
–How do you think the poet felt when he/she wrote the poem?
–Have you ever been in the same situation as the poet?

Questions about content
–Did you hear any new words?
–Do you think the poet was writing about something real or imaginary?
–What was the coolest part of the poem?
–Did you notice a specific style of poetry?
–What was the overall theme of the poem?
–Do you like this style of poetry?
–Would you have ended the poem the same?

Questions about values/morals
–What is this poem trying to teach us?
–Do you agree with the poet's point of view?
–Does this poem align with your family's values?
–How can this poem influence your decisions?

Questions that will work for any poem
–Why do you like or dislike this poem?
–What does this poem make you think of?
–Did you hear any words that were new to you?

Teachers Deeper Understanding

Looking closer at the poetry forms included in the poetry writing lessons

Understanding the Haiku

The haiku has its origins in Japan and is a traditional form of Japanese poetry. It evolved from collaborative linked-verse poetry called "renga" and its shortened form, "hokku." It is organized by morea (syllables or beats) and follows a very distinct rhythm. See the more detailed description about how mora work in the provided lesson.

Renga:
- Renga was a collaborative form of poetry in which poets took turns composing alternating three-line and two-line stanzas. The opening stanza, known as "hokku," often set the tone for the entire poem.

Hokku:
- The hokku, or starting verse, began to gain prominence as an independent form. It typically consisted of three lines with a 5-7-5 syllable pattern, capturing a moment in nature.

Development of Haiku:
- Over time, the hokku became a standalone form of poetry, and its structure evolved. The focus shifted from seasonal and nature themes to a broader range of subjects. The term "haiku" became more commonly used to describe this form in the 19th century.

Matsuo Bashō:
- Matsuo Bashō (1644–1694), one of the most famous Japanese poets, played a significant role in popularizing and refining the haiku. His haiku are renowned for their simplicity, depth, and focus on nature.

Influence of Zen Buddhism:
- Zen Buddhism had a profound impact on the development of haiku, emphasizing mindfulness, simplicity, and capturing the essence of a moment. Haiku, with its concise and contemplative nature, aligns well with Zen principles.

Masaoka Shiki:

- Masaoka Shiki (1867–1902) further contributed to the development of haiku by advocating for the inclusion of contemporary and everyday language. He also emphasized the importance of capturing the present moment.

Today, haiku has become a widely appreciated form of poetry globally. It typically consists of three lines with a 5-7-5 syllable pattern, though contemporary haiku often deviate from strict syllable counts. Haiku continues to embody the spirit of simplicity, observation of nature, and the fleeting beauty of moments.

Understanding Shape Poetry

Shape poetry, also known as concrete or visual poetry, has roots in ancient poetic traditions, but its formal recognition and development as a distinct genre occurred in the 20th century. Here's a brief overview of its origins:

Ancient Traditions:
- Elements of visual or concrete representation in poetry can be traced back to ancient cultures. For example, in ancient Greece, poems were sometimes written in specific shapes or patterns.

Calligrams:
- The idea of shaping poetry visually was further developed in medieval times, particularly with the concept of calligrams. Calligrams were poems or texts arranged in a way that visually represented their subject matter.

Apollinaire and Futurism:
- In the early 20th century, the French poet Guillaume Apollinaire experimented with visual poetry, creating poems that took on specific shapes on the page. This approach was influenced by the broader artistic movement of Futurism.

Dada Movement:
- The Dada movement, which emerged during World War I, embraced unconventional and avant-garde forms of art and poetry. Dadaists often used visual elements in their works, challenging traditional artistic norms.

E.E. Cummings:
- The American poet E.E. Cummings, in the early to mid-20th century, made significant contributions to shape poetry. He played with the arrangement of words on the page, experimenting with punctuation and form.

Concrete Poetry Movement:

- The term "concrete poetry" was coined in the 1950s, and the Concrete Poetry movement gained momentum in the 1950s and 1960s. Poets associated with this movement, such as Ian Hamilton Finlay and Augusto de Campos, explored the visual and spatial aspects of poetry.

Contemporary Influence:
- Contemporary poets continue to experiment with shape poetry, exploring the relationship between form and content. With advancements in digital media, poets have new opportunities to create interactive and dynamic shape poems.

Shape poetry, with its emphasis on the visual arrangement of words on the page, continues to be a dynamic and evolving form, offering poets a unique way to express themselves and engage readers visually and intellectually.

Understanding Acrostic Poetry

Acrostic poetry, a form of verse in which the first letters of each line or stanza spell out a word, name, or message when read in order, has ancient origins. The term "acrostic" itself comes from the Greek words "akros" (meaning "topmost" or "end") and "stichos" (meaning "line" or "verse"). Here are some key points about the origins of acrostic poetry:

Ancient Greece:
- Acrostic poems have roots in ancient Greek literature. The Greeks used acrostic patterns as a playful and creative way to enhance their poetry.

Classical Hebrew Poetry:
- The Hebrew Bible contains several examples of acrostic poems, most notably in the Book of Psalms and the Book of Lamentations. Psalms 119, for instance, consists of 22 sections, each corresponding to a letter of the Hebrew alphabet.

Latin and Medieval Literature:
- Acrostic poetry was also employed in Latin literature and later in medieval European literature. It became a popular form in various languages and cultures.

Riddles and Word Games:
- Acrostic poems were sometimes used as a form of riddle or word game. The challenge was to decipher the hidden message or name within the poem.

Renewed Interest in the Renaissance:

- During the Renaissance, there was a renewed interest in classical forms of poetry, including acrostics. Poets and writers of this era often used acrostic structures in their works.

Victorian Era and Romantic Period:
- The acrostic form experienced a resurgence in popularity during the Victorian era and the Romantic period. It was employed in both serious and playful contexts.

Modern Usage:
- Acrostic poetry continues to be a popular and versatile form used in various languages. It is often employed in educational settings as a creative writing exercise.

While acrostic poetry has ancient origins, its adaptability and playful nature have allowed it to persist through different literary traditions and time periods. Today, it remains a creative form that poets use to convey messages, names, or themes in a visually engaging way.

Poetry Styles & Terms

Alliteration—using a letters sound repetitively to create intrigue within a written work. Tongue twisters are a good example. Check out a Dr. Seuss book and look at all of the alliteration he uses.

Abecedarius poem— an acrostic, where the first word, strophe or verse appears in the order of the alphabet.

Acrostic—a word puzzle, poem or an composition where the letter at the beginning of each line spells a word or words.

Anaphora—using the same word or phrase over and over at the beginning or end of each line.

Blank Verse—poetry that is written with a meter, but without rhyming lines. It is almost always in Iambic Pentameter. John Milton's *Paradise Lost* is an entire epic poem that was written in blank verse.

Caesura—a pause that is made purposely. Usually, you know there is this pause because of punctuation. Things like dashes, slashes, and common punctuation. These usually appear in the middle of a line. Emily Dickinson loved to use caesura.

Couplet—a short, two-line verse. A couplet on its own creates a stanza.

Enjambment—there is no punctuation at the end of lines telling the reader not to stop. Instead, they are to read continuously without pause.

Free Verse—there are no rules to bind you when writing in free verse. There is no meter or rhyming unless the poet has chosen to do so. And even if they do they do not need to stick to it. It can be as long or as short as you would like. The poet is free to use alliteration, personification, and rhyme. "Fog" by Carl Sandburg is an example of free verse.

Foot—the name given to a unit or measurement in poetry. For example, a foot can represent two or three syllables. An iamb is the most common foot where it has two syllables and has a pattern of unstressed and stressed syllables.

Georgian Poets—there was a series of poem anthologies that were published by Harold Monro during the time of King George V. The poetry included in these anthologies are referred to as Georgian poets. There were five volumes published between 1912 and 1922. The style at the time was primarily romanticism, hedonism, and sentimentality.

Haiku—a Japanese form of poetry originally written about nature. A haiku has only three lines and follows a specific mora (syllable) pattern. The first line must have five mora, the second line must have seven mora and the third line has another five mora. The lines do not rhyme.

Iamb—a two syllable part of a complete meter. The first syllable being unstressed and the second being stressed. Another term for this is "a foot." The rhythm can be compared to a heartbeat.

Iambic Pentameter—a specific meter (rhythm) found in poetry. William Shakespeare is famous for his use of Iambic Pentameter. Each line has ten syllables which switch back and forth between stressed and unstressed syllables. There are five iambs in each line of the Iambic Pentameter. For those of you who are math minded: 2 syllables per iamb X 5 iambs per line = a 10-syllable line.

Internal Rhyme—where the rhyme happens in the center of a line.

Imagery—when a poet, or writer, uses words to create an image in the reader's mind. This includes metaphorical and figurative language.

Limerick—typically limericks are comical. They always have five lines. They follow a special rhyming pattern. The first, second and fifth line must rhyme and the third and fourth line have their own rhyme.

Lyric Poetry—Poetry that focuses on the feeling and thoughts of a single speaker. For instance, a poem expressing one's feelings of love or despair.

Meter—the pattern of beats (rhythm) within a line of poetry. Sometimes people will refer to the meter as a foot, or feet. It correlates with the number of feet in a line.
–Manometer has one foot
–Dimeter has two feet
–Trimeter has three feet

Monorhyme—when the ending rhyme sound of each line is the same.

Narrative Poetry—a poem that tells a story. They contain characters and have a beginning, middle, and end like a story. An example is Edgar Allen Poe's "The Raven."

Quatrain Poetry—a four-line poem or a four-lined stanza within a poem. They can use different rhyme scheme patterns.

Satire—the use of sarcasm, humor, mockery and exaggeration to make fun of people and/or society. It is a comical way to point out flaws and provoke a person or society to act and make a change. Techniques like exaggeration and irony are used to accomplish this. A caricature is a great visual example of satire.

Renku—a poem that is collaborated on with two or more poets. So much so that they even alternate who reads each alternating line. Each stanza must be self-standing. Each stanza may seem random, but there is supposed to be an association of some sort from one stanza to the next. There needs to be contrast from stanza to stanza. This style has many additional criteria that take practice to master.

Rhyme Schemes—it identifies the set pattern of rhyming for a particular poem. Rhyme schemes are represented by a set of capital letters. These letters can be used to identify which lines have matching rhymes. Rhyme Schemes that are often used are:
AAAA: each line ends with the same rhyme like Cat, Bat, Rat, Sat
ABAB: lines one and three rhyme and line two and four rhyme like play, phone, clay, stone

AABB: the first two lines rhyme and the second two lines rhyme like book, took, hair, care
ABCB: here only the second-and fourth-lines rhyme like flower, rain, daisy, pain

Romantic Poetry—scholars looking back in time to government, poetry, and art that they considered to be a virtuous time. A time of true nobility, poets tried to bring the style and grace of the Roman Era. So the term "Romantic" has to do with the Romans not love.

Shape Poetry—also known as concrete or visual poetry, is a form of poetry in which the visual arrangement of the text on the page is as important as its verbal meaning. In shape poetry, the words are intentionally arranged to create a visual representation of the subject matter, enhancing the overall impact of the poem. A poet who is known for his shape poetry is E. E. Cummings.

Shi fu— Shi means poetry in Chinese. Fu was a popular form of poetry during the Han dynasty. Fu means "rhapsody." Fu are parts of a poem that go into extreme extensive detail about a single place, person or detail. It also goes out of its way to use rare words. These poems were chanted, not sung. This style has been around since about 3 BCE.

Sonnet—a poem with fourteen lines and uses Iambic Pentameter. William Shakespeare is well known for his sonnets. The rhyme scheme typically used was ABAB CDCD EFEF GG.

Stanza—a grouping of lines.

Strophe—divisions within a poems structure containing stanzas with lines of varying length. This occurs often in free verse poetry and odes.

Syllable—this is a part of a word that only has a single beat or sound to it.

Tercet—a three lined poem or stanza.

Trochee—a foot opposite of the Iamb. Its syllables are stressed and then unstressed. An example of this is in the first line of William Bakes "The Tyger."

December

"No one is useless in this world who lightens the burdens of another."
-Charles Dickens

"When we give cheerfully and accept gratefully, everyone is blessed."
-Maya Angelou

"You have not lived today until you have done something for someone who can never repay you."
-John Bunyan

"Only a life lived for others is a life worthwhile."
-Albert Einstein

Winter

Storm
By Korbin Taylor

In the storm there comes the hail,
Wind and rain, and fearsome gales.
Awful raging left and right,
 Roaring storm all through the night.

---
gale— a current of air; a strong wind. The sense of this word is very indefinite. The poets use it in the sense of a moderate breeze of current of air

Winter
By Louisa May Alcott

The stormy winter's come at last,
With snow and rain and bitter blast;
Ponds and brooks are frozen o'er,
We cannot sail there any more.

The little birds are flown away
To warmer climes than ours;
They'll come no more till gentle May
Calls them back with flowers.

Oh, then the darling birds will sing
From their neat nests in the trees.
All creatures wake to welcome Spring,
And flowers dance in the breeze.

With patience wait till winter is o'er,
And all lovely things return;
Of every season try the more
Some knowledge or virtue to learn.

---
virtue— strength; that substance or quality of physical bodies, by which they act and produce effects on other bodies; bravery valor; Moral goodness; the practice of moral duties and the abstaining from vice

Mistress Winter
By Sophia Issac

Mistress Winter, Mistress Winter
Why is your heart so cold?
Why your hair so white
And skin so pale,
Your eyes ablaze
Blue like the frost filled lake,
A glimmering dress of ice,
A sparkling coat of snow?
Mistress Winter, Mistress Winter,
Why is your heart so cold?

Approach of Winter
By William Carlos Williams

The half-stripped trees
struck by a wind together,
bending all,
the leaves flutter drily
and refuse to let go
or driven like hail
stream bitterly out to one side
and fall
where the salvias, hard carmine,—
like no leaf that ever was—
edge the bare garden.

---
salvias—a plant that is a member of the mint family and cultivated for its tall clusters of flowers.
carmine— a powder or pigment, of a beautiful red or crimson color, bordering on purple, and used by painters in miniature, though rarely, on account of its great price.

A Tree In Winter
By Jeremiah Faustino

Day #1 of Winter
Brrr… Brrr… A gush of cold air hit my face.
Snow all over the place.
What is this? How to make it stop?
The temperature had dropped.
My best friend, Tulip, had withered,
My pal, Rose, had been caught in a blizzard.
I heard many voices cheer,
And realized Fall was no longer here.

Day #2 of Winter
My leaves had been replaced by crystals,
Each placed neatly on my arms.
My brother, Oak, had been dressed in icicles,
My birdfeeder had lost its charm.
Just a sapling; I'm not old but I have to be bold.
The challenges before me I'll surpass them all,
And prove to everyone that I'm not small!

Day #3 of Winter
Getting used to the cold; it bothers me no more!
I think I like this "Winter,"
Though the loss of my friends I still mourn.
But let's not leave this on a sour note,
For something else stayed afloat: Hope.

Day #4 of Winter
Snow covered everything I saw,
As I stood there gaping in awe.
I had awoken to a world of white,
As robins took off in flight.
My friends and I talk by sending letters on birds,
So, when I received one I savored every word.
It read: "Don't be sad. Winter isn't all that bad.
You can adapt to this new world. Your pal, Earl."

Day #5 of Winter
Soon I liked winter, with all its chilly demeanor,
My world became whiter, and my future brighter.

---

demeanor— behavior; carriage; deportment; how one is

Winter
By Walter De La Mare

   Clouded with snow
     The cold winds blow,
And shrill on leafless bough
The robin with its burning breast
     Alone sings now.

   The rayless sun,
     Day's journey done,
Sheds its last ebbing light
On fields in leagues of beauty spread
     Unearthly white.

   Thick draws the dark,
     And spark by spark,
The frost-fires kindle, and soon
Over that sea of frozen foam
     Floats the white moon.

---

shrill— sharp; acute; piercing; as sound
ebbing— flowing back; declining; decaying
bough— the branch of a tree; applied to a branch of size, not to a small shoot

Winter Moon
By Langston Hughes

How thin and sharp is the moon tonight!
How thin and sharp and ghostly white
Is the slim curved crook of the moon tonight!

Winter Voice
By Mala Sabapathy

Wake up earth and gaze upon the Winter.
Pools of white glitter crowd the Winter's land, with its playful sparkles and shines that glows in the morning's frosty haze.
Drifting snowflakes dance and sparkle before settling down to snow.
Look down to the lake, see the deep crystalline depths of ice that covers the waters flow.
Clouds cover the light blue sky as they dust icy forms all over this Winter.
The reflections of a pink puffy cloud ripples on the surface of water, yet to be frozen.
Sunset has arrived at last, orange paints the sky and reflects onto the icy snow that is now everywhere in sight.
Stars begin to glow, looking like little drifts of more snow against the purple and blue backdrop.
A cool night casting is set over our scene and the world seems to darken and waver.
Then out of our night blazes a light, blue and purple, pink and green, all the colours you've ever seen.
These rippling lights that dance across the sky, are the most beautiful thing, in my opinion, in our Winter's land.
Not even the moon can outshine such beauty, not even the sun can outshine this light.
Merry dancers, Angel dust, Aurora borealis, Northern lights, Foxfire, this glamor has many names, but no words can ever describe the song it gives us.
It waves its silky streaks across the sky against the dark night.
What a beauty this Winter is, everything seems to fill our hearts with wonder.
But I have one thing to ask you.
Something important to request.
Listen closely to the howling winds that sweep the land.

---

crystalline—having a crystal like structure made of crystals
aurora borealis—a natural electrical phenomenon that occurs at the poles of Earth creating waves of colored light from sun particles reacting with atoms in the upper atmosphere.

Spellbound
By Emily Brontë

The night is darkening round me,
The wild winds coldly blow;
But a tyrant spell has bound me
And I cannot, cannot go.
The giant trees are bending
Their bare boughs weighed with snow.
And the storm is fast descending,
And yet I cannot go.
Clouds beyond clouds above me,
Wastes beyond wastes below;
But nothing drear can move me;
I will not, cannot go.

---

bough— The branch of a tree; applied to a branch of size, not to a small shoot.

Jack Frost
By Gabriel Setoun (Given Name-Thomas Nicoll Hepburn)

The door was shut, as doors should be,
 Before you went to bed last night;
Yet Jack Frost has got in, you see,
 And left your window silver white.

He must have waited till you slept;
 And not a single word he spoke,
But pencilled o'er the panes and crept
 Away again before you woke.

And now you cannot see the hills
 Nor fields that stretch beyond the lane;
But there are fairer things than these
 His fingers traced on every pane.

Rocks and castles towering high;
 Hills and dales, and streams and fields;
And knights in armor riding by,
 With nodding plumes and shining shields.

And here are little boats, and there
 Big ships with sails spread to the breeze;
And yonder, palm trees waving fair
 On islands set in silver seas,

And butterflies with gauzy wings;
 And herds of cows and flocks of sheep;
And fruit and flowers and all the things
 You see when you are sound asleep.

For, creeping softly underneath
 The door when all the lights are out,
Jack Frost takes every breath you breathe,
 And knows the things you think about.

He paints them on the window-pane
 In fairy lines with frozen steam;
And when you wake you see again
 The lovely things you saw in dream.

---
dale— a low place between hills; a vale or valley.

Activity

Koch Fractal Snowflake Activity

Can you name the tune that this quote is from? "...frozen fractals all around."
If you said Disney's Frozen then you are correct. Snowflakes are a fractal you can find in nature and this is because if a snowflake has the chance to develop in a stable environment it will have six identical limbs. A fractal has a repeating pattern that progressively gets smaller.

A Koch snowflake is a famous fractal shape. Start with an equilateral triangle and add smaller equilateral triangles to each side. Repeat the process, making each iteration smaller. The result is a snowflake with a self-similar pattern. Typically, the triangle is shrunk down to 1/3 of its size each time.

1. Draw a big equilateral triangle, a triangle with three equal sides.
2. Using small dots, divide each side of the triangle into three equal parts.
3. Use the two dots as your starting and ending points to draw the next triangle

Alternative: You can print off the following page and color each size triangle a certain color of choice. You can even try to add more triangles

Who is Koch?
Swedish mathematician Niels Fabian Helge von Koch. He was born on January 25, 1870, and was a prominent mathematician known for his work in number theory and geometry.

Niels Koch introduced the Koch Snowflake, which is a well-known mathematical curve and one of the earliest fractal curves to be described. The Koch Snowflak's self-replication results in a curve with an infinite perimeter but in a limited space.

Koch's contributions to mathematics extend beyond fractals, and he made significant contributions to the study of number theory and more. The Koch Snowflake, however, remains one of his most enduring and visually intriguing contributions to the world of mathematics.

Other kinds of fractals to learn about

Tree Fractal
Mandelbrot set fractal
Newton fractal
Fibonacci fractal
Sierpiński triangle fractal
Dragon Curve fractal

Koch Snow Fractal

Hanukkah

The Power of Brotherhood & Faith
By Amanda Schenkenberger

In days of old, in a land of faith and strife,
A tale of courage, in the darkest of life.
A band of brothers, steadfast and bold,
Fought for their freedom, their story told.

Desecrated was the sacred temple's core,
Pigs bloodshed stained its hallowed floor,
Yet the spirit of light, deep in their soul,
Ignited their purpose, a righteous goal.

They rose against the might of the foe,
With faith in their hearts, they'd overthrow.
Miraculously, a candle's flame did burn,
Through days and nights, their heart's concern.

The oil, so scarce, was meant to wane,
But the light kept burning, a divine refrain.
For eight days and nights, the flame did shine,
A symbol of hope, in a time so malign.

The temple was purified, honor restored,
Their faith in God, together, they poured.
In the face of darkness, their light did play,
Now we remember brothers and faith each Hanukkah day.

Chanukah Dreams
By Judith Ish-Kishor

Chanukah I think most dear
Of the feasts of all the year.
I could sit and watch all night
Every twinkling baby light.

Father lights the first one—green;
Hope it always seems to mean;
Hope and Strength to glow anew
In the heart of every Jew.

Jacob lights the blue for Truth.
Pink for Love is lit by Ruth.
Then the white one falls to me,
White that shines for Purity.

How the story of those days
Fills my wondering heart with praise!
And in every flame one sees
The heroic Maccabees.

Miracles
by Walt Whitman
Why, who makes much of a miracle?
As to me I know of nothing else but miracles,
Whether I walk the streets of Manhattan,
Or dart my sight over the roofs of houses toward the sky,
Or wade with naked feet along the beach just in the edge of the water,
Or stand under trees in the woods,
Or talk by day with any one I love, or sleep in the bed at night with any one I love,
Or sit at table at dinner with the rest,
Or look at strangers opposite me riding in the car,
Or watch honey-bees busy around the hive of a summer forenoon,
Or animals feeding in the fields,
Or birds, or the wonderfulness of insects in the air,
Or the wonderfulness of the sundown, or of stars shining so quiet and bright,
Or the exquisite delicate thin curve of the new moon in spring;
These with the rest, one and all, are to me miracles,
The whole referring, yet each distinct and in its place.
To me every hour of the light and dark is a miracle,
Every cubic inch of space is a miracle,
Every square yard of the surface of the earth is spread with the same,
Every foot of the interior swarms with the same.
To me the sea is a continual miracle,
The fishes that swim—the rocks—the motion of the waves—the
    ships with men in them,
What stranger miracles are there?

Activity

Traditional Sufganiyot Cooking Activity

Sufganiyot, which are jelly-filled doughnuts typically eaten during the Jewish festival of Hanukkah, have their origins in Jewish culinary traditions. The exact origin of sufganiyot is not definitively known. It may originate from the Jewish communities of Eastern Europe or adopted in Germany by the Ashkenazi Jews who immigrated from Germany to Isreal.

The tradition of eating fried foods during Hanukkah is linked to the miracle of the oil that occurred in the Second Temple of Jerusalem. According to the Hanukkah story, when the Maccabees rededicated the temple after their victory over the Seleucid Greeks, there was only enough oil to light the menorah for one day. Miraculously, the oil lasted for eight days, symbolizing the duration of the celebration of Hanukkah.

The association with fried foods, including sufganiyot, comes from the practice of cooking in oil to commemorate this miracle. Sufganiyot are particularly popular in Israel, where they are filled with various sweet fillings such as jelly, custard, or chocolate, and dusted with powdered sugar. The tradition of enjoying sufganiyot during Hanukkah has since spread to Jewish communities around the world.

Sufganiyot (soof-gaa-nee-owt)
Yields 1 dozen
NF

Ingredients
- 3 cups white bread flour + extra
- 1 tsp salt
- 1 envelope dry active yeast (2½ tsp)
- 3/4 cup lukewarm milk
- 2 tbsp sugar + extra
- 2 large eggs
- 2 tbsp butter, melted and cooled
- vegetable oil for frying
- 1 jar of your favorite jam
- cinnamon or powdered sugar for dusting

Instructions

1. stir together 2 tbsp of warm milk and 2 tbsp of sugar. Then add the dry active yeast and let sit , 5 minutes until foamy.
2. Combined 3 cups flour and 1 tsp salt in a mixing bowl. Mix in the yeast mixture. Add the eggs and butter to the flour mixture. And mix until it is crumbly.
3. Add the rest of the milk, 1 tbsp at a time until it forms a ball of dough.
4. On a lightly floured surface, knead the dough until it is smooth. Place into a greased bowl, cover with a towel, and cover with a bowl and let rise for two hours until doubled in size.
5. Punch down the risen dough. Turn out onto a lightly floured surface.
6. With a lightly floured rolling pin, roll out the dough to ½" thick. If the dough sticks then dust the rolling pin lightly.
7. Cut 3-4" rounds with a lightly floured biscuit cutter or cup. combine the scraps and reroll to make more rounds. OR to make it easier, you can cut the dough into 3 inch squares.
8. Place each sufganiyot onto a lightly floured baking sheets with parchment paper leaving room for then to rise. Cover and let them rise in a warm spot for 30 minutes.
9. Heat a deep, heavy pot filled 3" high with vegetable oil (avocado and grapeseed oil would also work). Heat it to 350° F (175°C).
10. Gently transfer the risen sufganiyot a few at a time and cook until golden and puffed. About 1-2 minutes each side.
11. Prepare a plate with 2-3 cups of mixed sugar and cinnamon or powdered sugar. Prepare a second plate with a couple layers of paper towels.
12. Carefully lift the doughnuts from the oil using a slotted spoon and blot briefly on the paper towels. While sufganiyot are still hot, roll or sprinkle with cinnamon-sugar Set donuts aside to cool
13. Fill a pastry bag (1/4" round tip) or a zip-top bag with the corner cut off with jam. Insert the tip into the top of each sufganiyot and fill with about 1-2 tbsp of jam.

Nana Tea Making Activity

Nana Mint, also known as Spearmint, is a type of mint that is often used to make herbal teas. It is known for its refreshing and slightly sweet flavor. The term "Nana" is sometimes associated with a specific type of mint tea popular in the Middle East.

Ingredients

- 1 tsp Nana (spearmint)
- ½ tsp chamomile flowers
- 1 tsp lemon verbena
- Slices lemon

Instructions

1. Boil your water
2. Add water to cup
3. Place herbs into a tea ball or strait into your cup
4. Let steep for 10 minutes.
5. Remove tea ball or strain tea.
6. Add your sliced lemon and enjoy

Legendary Lights
By Alter Ableson

O, the legendary light,
Gleaming goldenly in night
    Like the stars above,
Beautiful, like lights in dream,
Eight, the taper-flames that stream
    All one glory and one love.

In our Temple, magical—
Memories, now tragical—
Holy hero-hearts aflame
With a glory more than fame;
There where a shrine is every sod,
    Every grave, God's golden ore,
With a paean whose rhyme to God,
    Lit these lamps of yore.

Lights, you are a living dream,
Faith and bravery you beam,
    Youth and dawn and May.
Would your beam were more than dream,
Would the light and love you stream,
    Stirred us, spurred us, aye!

Fabled memories of flame,
Till the beast in man we tame,
Tyrants bow to truth, amain,
Brands and bullets yield to brain,
Guns to God, and shells to soul,
Hounds to heart resign the role,
Pillared lights of liberty,
In your fairy flames, we'll see
Faith's and freedom's Phoenix-might,
The Omnipotence of Right.

Children in Winter

What Is Winter?
By Kiralee Larsen

Winter is the falling snow
The magic in the air.
Winter is the hot cocoa
We like to sip and share.

Winter is the sledding fun
Out on the rolling hills.
Winter is the carolers
And their melodic trills.

Winter is the skiing that
I've never done myself.
Winter is the cozy books
That wait upon my shelf.

Winter is the snowy days
I sit beside a fire.
Winter is the Christmas songs,
The tunes that never tire.

Winter is the figure eights
That never seem to end.
Winter is the snowball fights
I have with lots of friends.

Winter is so many things
Like candles, wreaths, and more.
I'm so glad I've had a lot
Of winters to explore.

---
melodic—to have or produce a melody
trill— a shake of the voice in singing, or of the sound of an instrument

Three Little Kittens
By Mother Goose

The three little kittens, they lost their mittens,
And they began to cry,
"Oh, mother dear, we sadly fear,
That we have lost our mittens."
"What!   Lost your mittens, you naughty kittens!
Then you shall have no pie."
"Meow, meow, meow."
"Then you shall have no pie."

The three little kittens, they found their mittens,
And they began to cry,
"Oh, mother dear, see here, see here,
For we have found our mittens."
"Put on your mittens, you silly kittens,
And you shall have some pie."
"Purr, purr, purr,
Oh, let us have some pie."

The three little kittens put on their mittens,
And soon ate up the pie,
"Oh, mother dear, we greatly fear,
That we have soiled our mittens."
"What, soiled your mittens, you naughty kittens!"
Then they began to sigh,
"Meow, meow, meow,"
Then they began to sigh.

The three little kittens, they washed their mittens,
And hung them out to dry,
"Oh, mother dear, do you not hear,
That we have washed our mittens?"
"What, washed your mittens, then you're good kittens,
But I smell a rat close by."
"Meow, meow, meow,
We smell a rat close by."

A Wish Of When
By Christine Owens

I wish I had a fireplace when I was a small child
I dreamt of sitting there in front of flames dancing so mild
I would have hung red stockings there like seen in all the books
I wanted to know Santa Clause could come in and take looks
Of the small tree and modest home that I was living in
And see how much we would appreciate the gifts from him
My brother and I would have sat and held each other tight
And soaked in all the peaceful silence when we woke at night
We would whisper all our plans we'd play at break of day
And giggle about silly jokes we'd whisper, warm at play
It would have been so nice to have a fireplace back then
All these dreams would have been real and not a wish of when.

Sneezles
By A.A. Milne

Christopher Robin
Had wheezles
And sneezles,
They bundled him
Into
His bed.
They gave him what goes
With a cold in the nose,
And some more for a cold
In the head.
They wondered
If wheezles
Could turn
Into measles,
If sneezles
Would turn
Into mumps;
They examined his chest
For a rash,
And the rest
Of his body for swellings and lumps.
They sent for some doctors
In sneezles
And wheezles
To tell them what ought
To be done.
All sorts and conditions
Of famous physicians
Came hurrying round
At a run.
They all made a note
Of the state of his throat,
They asked if he suffered from thirst;
They asked if the sneezles
Came after the wheezles,
Or if the first sneezle
Came first.
They said, "If you teazle

A sneezle
Or wheezle,
A measle
May easily grow.
But humour or pleazle
The wheezle
Or sneezle,
The measle
Will certainly go."
They expounded the reazles
For sneezles
And wheezles,
The manner of measles
When new.
They said "If he freezles
In draughts and in breezles,
Then PHTHEEZLES
May even ensue."

Christopher Robin
Got up in the morning,
The sneezles had vanished away.
And the look in his eye
Seemed to say to the sky,
"Now, how to amuse them to-day?"

Smiling Girls, Rosy Boys
By Mother Goose

Smiling girls, rosy boys,
Come and buy my little toys;
Monkeys made of gingerbread,
And sugar horses painted red.

Saint Nicholas
By Richard Hunter

   Saint Nicholas brings presents
      For little girls and boys;
   Saint Nicholas brings dozens
      Of all the nicest toys.

   Hang out your biggest stocking
      Before you go to sleep;
   But if you hear him coming,
      You mustn't even peep.

Winter Treats

Sticky Licking Peppermint
By Christine Owens

Do you remember eating candy canes when you were young?
The wrapper pulled back carefully by mother then begun
Your licking, slurping, tongue at work, your lips puckered up tight
To capture every sweet slick taste of peppermint delight
Your cheeks start to get sticky, somehow out to your ear
Your hair has gotten tangled and you start to have some fear
You tug it off so carefully, your stick you will not break
But then your hair is on your forehead and there is no mistake
Finishing this sugar cane is worth discomfort so…..
You put it in your other hand and go and go and go.

Activity

Peppermint Ornaments Craft Activity

This craft is super simple, looks good, and barely costs any money. Any age can do it and it would make cute decorations for your Christmas tree or a class room tree.

Materials: Red and White pipe cleaners

Instructions
1. Set a red and white pipe cleaner next to each other
2. Twist them around each other
3. Fold the tip on each end over to hold it in place
4. Bend the top like a candy cane.

*Another variation: provide red and white tri beads and slide them onto a ½ piece of pipe cleaner alternating colors every 2 beads. Bend the tip of the pipe cleaner before threading. Once it is almost full you will fold over the open end to close it off. Bend it into a candy cane shape and you are done.

Peppermint Pillows Cooking Activity

Peppermint sticks date back to at least the 17th century and are enjoyed by all ages to this day. These peppermint pillows are a simpler way for you to make a peppermint treat at home or in the classroom. No cooking involved.

Ingredients
- 4 ¾ cup powdered sugar
- 2 Tbsp heavy cream
- 8 Tbsp butter
- 1 tsp peppermint extract or peppermint essential oils
- Food coloring (optional

Instructions
1. Remove you butter from the fridge about 20 minutes before you start
2. Mix together the butter, powdered sugar, extract or 1-2 drop of essential oil
3. Keep mixing till you have a nice white dough

4. If you want to color them you will divide them now and add the colors to each portion. Kneed in until the color is even.
5. Roll the dough into snake like ropes that are ½ inch thick and lay them on a parchment covered cookie sheet. Now cut the snakes into ½ inch pieces and let them air dry over night.
6. Store them in an open container. An air tight container will result in them becoming soft again.

When Good King Arthur Ruled The Land
By Mother Goose

When good king Arthur ruled this land,
He was a goodly king;
He stole three pecks of barley-meal,
To make a bag-pudding.

A bag-pudding the king did make,
And stuffed it well with plums:
And in it put great lumps of fat,
As big as my two thumbs.

The king and queen did eat thereof,
And noblemen beside;
And what they could not eat that night,
The queen next morning fried.

Handy Spandy Jack-a-Dandy
By Mother Goose

Handy spandy Jack-a-dandy
Loves plum cake and sugar candy,
He bought some at the grocers shop
And out he came, hop, hop, hop.

Catching Chocolate
By Kiralee Larsen

I have a cup of chocolate,
It's nice and warm and hot.
I take a sip,
My hand---it slips!
The cup I barely caught.

Activity

Home Made Hot Cocoa Cooking Activity

Don't drop your cup of cocoa!
Don't worry, you won't loosen your grip from this
perfect cup of chocolate. Take a few sips and read a couple poems
for a cozy activity. What is your favorite winter poem?
The Aztecs, around 2,000 years ago, created a frothy and bitter beverage using ground cocoa beans, water, and spices like chili peppers. They believed it had special powers and used it in religious ceremonies. Later, in Europe, people started to add sugar to the drink.

Ingredients
- ¾ cup granulated sugar
- 1/3 cup unsweetened cocoa powder
- Pinch of salt
- 1/3 cup boiling water
- 3 ½ cups milk
- ¾ tsp vanilla extract
- Heavy cream, half and half, or milk
- *Milk Chocolate Chips (optional)
- Marshmallows (optional)

Instructions
1. Add the sugar, cocoa, and salt to a sauce pan and add the boiling water. Whisk until it is dissolved.
2. Bring to a simmer and whisk constantly for two minutes
3. Stir in the milk and then remove from the heat.
4. Stir in the vanilla
5. Pour the cocoa evenly into the mugs and top off with the heavy cream

*If you want to add even more chocolatey goodness to your cup add a tablespoon chocolate chips to the cocoa filled cup and stir till they are dissolved. If you don't plan on serving your cocoa piping hot in the cup, then add the chocolate chips to the pan once your have removed it from the heat and stir it in.

Polly Put The Kettle On
By Mother Goose

Polly put the kettle on,
Polly put the kettle on,
Polly put the kettle on,
We'll all have tea.

Sukey take it off again,
Sukey take it off again,
Sukey take it off again,
They've all gone away.

Little Jack Horner
By Mother Goose

Little Jack Horner
Sat in the corner,
Eating his Christmas pie;
He put in his thumb,
And pulled out a plum,
And said, "What a good boy am I!"

Christmas

The Christmas Tree
By Josephine Preston Peabody

I know you're in the house;
I know you are in there;
I feel the green and breathing
All around the air.
I know you're safe and warm;
  I know you're very near.
    Oh, darling Tree,
      Do you hear?

I promised not to look
(The way I did before),
But I can hear you purring--
Purring, through the door:
A green, soft, purring;
  Just as if you knew:
    Everybody here
      Loves you.

Don't feel lonely,
Now you are in-doors.--
Wait for all the shining things
To-morrow,--all yours!
Then you won't know what to think!--
  All over Candle-light.
    --Oh, darling Tree,
      Good-night.

And I love you, I love you;
And everybody, too.
And so does the market-man
That brought us you!
And if you haven't Anything
  For me, this year,
    --I love you. Good-night!
      Do you hear?

Like A Twinkling Tannenbaum
By Sharon Dodd

Just like a twinkling Tannenbaum,
The word's a sight to see.
The rivers are her garland strands,
Her shine, the glassy seas.

The mounts and hills are her big bows,
She wears them merrily.
The clouds, her snow-white powder frost,
Her scent is forestry.

And something else adorns this gem,
The ornaments galore.
That's each and every one of us,
For we're unique decor.

Tannenbaum—German for Christmas Tree

Across Delaware
By Will Carleton
(On Washington crossing the Delaware on Christmas Day)

The winter night is cold and drear,
Along the river's sullen flow;
The cruel frost is camping here —
The air has living blades of snow.
Look! pushing from the icy strand,
With ensigns freezing in the air,
There sails a small but mighty band,
Across the dang'rous Delaware.

---
ensign—a flag or banner; a figured cloth or piece of silk, attached to a staff, and usually with figures, colors or arms thereon

Snow and Snow
By Matsuo Basho

The snow and snow.
This evening would have
The great moon of December

Gifts At Christmas
By Emilee Larsen
HAIKU

Wrapped in red and green.
Delight to open and see.
Lights on Christmas tree.

Activity

Haiku Fun Poetry Writing Activity

Materials: paper and pencil

A haiku is a special kind of poem that comes from Japan. It's like a tiny snapshot of nature or a moment in time. A haiku has three lines with a specific number of syllables in each line—
5 syllables in the first line, 7 syllables in the second line, and 5 syllables in the third line.

Haikus often capture the beauty of the world around us, like a blooming flower, a buzzing insect, or a quiet snowfall. They help us pay attention to the small, wonderful things in nature and let us share those moments with others in a short and sweet way!
When haikus are translated into English they typically don't have the correct number of syllables, the intended rhythm of a haiku. In its original form the poem is said to a set amount of beats or morea, like music. 3 lines with 8 beats. Some morea (beats) are spoken in and some are left silent. Look at the haiku below written by Matsuo Basho. The morae, or "syllables", have been broken up into the correct rhythm. Try to write your own haiku or try to write the poem in Japanese characters.

Yki to yuki/ Koyoi shiwasu no/ Meigetsu ya

雪と雪 今宵師走の 名月か

The Christmas Wreath
By Anna de Brémont

Oh! Christmas wreath upon the wall,
    Within thine ivied space
I see the years beyond recall,
    Amid thy leaves I trace
The shadows of a happy past,
    When all the world was bright,
And love its magic splendour cast
    O'er morn and noon and night.

Oh! Christmas wreath upon the wall,
    'Neath memory's tender spell
A wondrous charm doth o'er thee fall,
    And round thy beauty dwell.
Thine ivy hath the satiny sheen
    Of tresses I've caressed,
Thy holly's crimson gleam I've seen
    On lips I oft have pressed.

Oh! Christmas wreath upon the wall,
    A mist steals o'er my sight.
Dear hallow'd wreath, these tears are all
    The pledge I now can plight
To those loved ones whose spirit eyes
    Shine down the flight of time;
Around God's throne their voices rise
    To swell the Christmas Chime!

Dark Night Caroling
By Christine Owens

I took my children caroling one cold dark winter night
Throughout the streets in Michigan and wondered at the site
One family snuck and flipped the switch to turn off all their lights
Another peeked out windows as if we were quite the fright

Many seemed so dark and lonely, had nobody home
But we kept going caroling and didn't stop our roam

But there was a magic moment that we did not expect
We stoped at a young families home thinking they would reject
But lo' they opened windows and they came up to the door
Tears filled up the mother's eyes and they began to poor
"I've never seen real caroling" the mother said out loud
My children and I, satisfied, went home feeling so proud.

Christmas
By Jeremiah Faustino

Covered in a blanket of warmth,
As I sip at my hot cocoa happily,
And stare at the line of gifts,
And look at the decorated tree.

The merry cheer the Christmas brings,
Is not so easily quenched,
It is a season of great celebration!
Where in happiness we are drenched.

The jolly stories and presents,
Joyful hollers fill the air,
Up in the endless darkness,
One star shines up there.

Snow falls, kissing the ground,
Not a bare spot to be found.
Piles of snow white as a dove,
Mounds of ice staring above.

Lights green and red beam with delight,
Holiday cheer at every sight!
The grass is nowhere to be seen,
Everything looks sparkling clean!

Candy canes and elves galore,
Out of stock in every store!
Children big and small,
Gape at the brightness of it all!

But let us not be quick to forget,
What TRULY makes Christmas a joy,
'Tis the day we pause to give honor,
To the birth of our Savior, Christ the Lord!

Christmas Bells
By Henry Wadsworth Longfellow

I heard the bells on Christmas Day
Their old, familiar carols play,
    And wild and sweet
    The words repeat
Of peace on earth, good-will to men!

And thought how, as the day had come,
The belfries of all Christendom
    Had rolled along
    The unbroken song
Of peace on earth, good-will to men!

Till, ringing, singing on its way,
The world revolved from night to day,
    A voice, a chime,
    A chant sublime
Of peace on earth, good-will to men!

Then from each black, accursed mouth
The cannon thundered in the South,
    And with the sound
    The carols drowned
Of peace on earth, good-will to men!

It was as if an earthquake rent
The hearth-stones of a continent,
    And made forlorn
    The households born
Of peace on earth, good-will to men!

And in despair I bowed my head;
"There is no peace on earth," I said:
    "For hate is strong,
    And mocks the song
Of peace on earth, good-will to men!"

Then pealed the bells more loud and deep:

"God is not dead; nor doth he sleep!
   The Wrong shall fail,
   The Right prevail,
With peace on earth, good-will to men!"

Christendom— The territories, countries or regions inhabited by Christians; those who believe in Christ; Christianity

sublime— grandeur; beauty that causes awe

rent— a break or breach made by force

forlorn— Deserted; destitute; stripped or deprived; forsaken. Hence, lost; helpless; wretched

mock— To deride; to laugh at; to ridicule; to treat with scorn or contempt.

Religious Christmas

Christmastide
By Christina Rossetti

Love came down at Christmas,
   Love all lovely, Love Divine;
Love was born at Christmas,
   Star and Angels gave the sign.

Worship we the Godhead,
   Love Incarnate, Love Divine;
Worship we our Jesus:
   But wherewith for sacred sign?

Love shall be our token,
   Love be yours and love be mine,
Love to God and all men,
   Love for plea and gift and sign.

---

incarnate—embodied in flesh; invested in the flesh

Carol Of The Russian Children
Russian Folk Song

Snow-bound mountains, snow-bound valleys,
Snow-bound plateaus, clad in white,
Fur-robed moujiks, fur-robed nobles,
Fur-robed children, see the light.
Shaggy pony, shaggy oxen,
Gentle shepherds wait the light;
Little Jesus, little Mother,
Good St. Joseph, come this night.

December 25, 1914
By Anders Angle

An icy gust slices into my otherworldly lair.
Gunshots and powder will fill the air.
Tanks will come rolling, the men must prepare to fight,
I squeal, so giddy, so full of delight,
I will emerge to collect souls as to the lifeless ground they fall,
I'll feast on the sound of death's silent caterwaul,
I'll devour the men who aren't lucky enough to live,
They'll bleed and they'll die and have nothing left to give.
I'll lick my lips and I'll feed on their screams,
I am terror and I am death, I am the stuff of dreams.

I slither quietly from my cavernous pit,
And see something frightening, I have to admit,
It's terrifying, and the reason for which I cannot assume,
There are no souls for me to consume.
Through the foggy air, I see the fighting has stopped,
There's no death or wailing in sight and my heart has dropped.

I fly at the nearest soldier, I'm curious.
I scream at him, "Man, this lack of destruction is making me furious!"
He glances right at me, and his countenance shifts,
He looks at the ground, then his strong chin lifts,
His jaw is set, his eyes are stone,
He whispers, "We are cold and wet, please leave us alone."

I laugh and he flinches, such a small insignificant thing,
I can see that he's tired; he'll soon feel death's sting.
The man stands up—I am shocked by his faithful soul,
I feel an unseen power pulling me back into my malicious hole.

The man begins to sob icy tears of relief,
This little cold man with infallible belief.

"I name thee Satan, now get thee away,

I see you are hungry, but this is Baby Jesus' day."
___
countenance—how one appears; air; look; appearance of the face; Favor; good will; kindness
insignificant— void of signification; destitute of meaning
malicious— harboring ill will or enmity; proceeding from extreme hatred or ill will

Cradle Hymn
By Martin Luther

Away in a manger, no crib for a bed,
The little Lord Jesus laid down his sweet head.
The stars in the bright sky looked down where he lay—
The little Lord Jesus asleep on the hay.
The cattle are lowing, the baby awakes,
But little Lord Jesus, no crying he makes.
I love thee, Lord Jesus! Look down from the sky,
And stay by my cradle till morning is nigh.

Carol
By William Canton

When the herds were watching
    In the midnight chill,
Came a spotless lambkin
    From the heavenly hill.

Snow was on the mountains,
    And the wind was cold,
When from God's own garden
    Dropped a rose of gold.

When 'twas bitter winter,
    Houseless and forlorn
In a star-lit stable
    Christ the Babe was born.

Welcome, heavenly lambkin;
    Welcome, golden rose;
Alleluia, Baby,
    In the swaddling clothes!

The Three Kings
By Henry Wadsworth Longfellow

Three Kings came riding from far away,
   Melchior and Gaspar and Baltasar;
Three Wise Men out of the East were they,
And they travelled by night and they slept by day,
   For their guide was a beautiful, wonderful star.

The star was so beautiful, large, and clear,
   That all the other stars of the sky
Became a white mist in the atmosphere,
And by this they knew that the coming was near
   Of the Prince foretold in the prophecy.

Three caskets they bore on their saddle-bows,
   Three caskets of gold with golden keys;
Their robes were of crimson silk with rows
Of bells and pomegranates and furbelows,
   Their turbans like blossoming almond-trees.

And so the Three Kings rode into the West,
   Through the dusk of night, over hill and dell,
And sometimes they nodded with beard on breast
And sometimes talked, as they paused to rest,
   With the people they met at some wayside well.

"Of the child that is born," said Baltasar,
   "Good people, I pray you, tell us the news;
For we in the East have seen his star,
And have ridden fast, and have ridden far,
   To find and worship the King of the Jews."

And the people answered, "You ask in vain;
   We know of no king but Herod the Great!"
They thought the Wise Men were men insane,
As they spurred their horses across the plain,
   Like riders in haste, and who cannot wait.

And when they came to Jerusalem,
   Herod the Great, who had heard this thing,

Sent for the Wise Men and questioned them;
And said, "Go down unto Bethlehem,
   And bring me tidings of this new king."

So they rode away; and the star stood still,
   The only one in the gray of morn
Yes, it stopped, it stood still of its own free will,
Right over Bethlehem on the hill,
   The city of David where Christ was born.

And the Three Kings rode through the gate and the guard,
   Through the silent street, till their horses turned
And neighed as they entered the great inn-yard;
But the windows were closed, and the doors were barred,
   And only a light in the stable burned.

And cradled there in the scented hay,
   In the air made sweet by the breath of kine,
The little child in the manger lay,
The child, that would be king one day
   Of a kingdom not human but divine.

His mother Mary of Nazareth
   Sat watching beside his place of rest,
Watching the even flow of his breath,
For the joy of life and the terror of death
   Were mingled together in her breast.

They laid their offerings at his feet:
   The gold was their tribute to a King,
The frankincense, with its odor sweet,
Was for the Priest, the Paraclete,
   The myrrh for the body's burying.

And the mother wondered and bowed her head,
   And sat as still as a statue of stone;
Her heart was troubled yet comforted,
Remembering what the Angel had said
   Of an endless reign and of David's throne.

Then the Kings rode out of the city gate,

>   With a clatter of hoofs in proud array;
>   But they went not back to Herod the Great,
>   For they knew his malice and feared his hate,
>   And returned to their homes by another way.

kine—plural for cows; more than one cow

Paraclete— an advocate; one called to aid or support; hence, the consoler, comforter or intercessor, a term applied to the Holy Spirit.

malice— a disposition to injure others without cause, from mere personal gratification or from a spirit of revenge; unprovoked malignity or spite.

December Poetry Writing Prompts

Write a poem about see snow for the first time

Write a poem about a Christmas in a warm place

Write a poem about Santa Clause

Write a poem about Saint Nichols

Write a poem about a dreidel

Write a poem about a snow blizzard

Write a poem about baby Jesus in a manger

Write a poem about Christmas Eve

Write about poem to Santa

Write a poem about reindeer

Write a poem about snow crystals

Write a poem about Christmas music

December Vocabulary Cards

*Download your **FREE**
Vocabulary Flashcards at
www.AYearofPoetryTeaTime.com/shop
And use the code "WINTER" at checkout.*

SELECT DECEMBER VOCABULARY

malice Storm By Korbin Taylor pg.34	a disposition to injure others without cause; unprovoked
gale Storm By Korbin Taylor pg.34	a current of air; a strong wind
virtue Winter By Louisa May Alcott pg.34	moral goodness; strength; that substance or quality of physical bodies.
demeanor A Tree In Winter By Jeremiah Faustino pg.36	behavior; carriage; deportment; how one is
ebbing Winter By Walter De La Mare pg.37	flowing back; declining; decaying
bough Winter By Walter De La Mare pg.37 Spellbound By Emily Brontë pg.39 The Fairies' Nook in Winter By Rhylin Taylor pg.169	the branch of a tree; applied to a branch of size, not to a small shoot.

December Vocabulary words, Copy, cut out, fold on the dashed line, and glue together to make flash cards

SELECT DECEMBER VOCABULARY

countenance December 25, 1914 By Anders Angle pg.72	how one appears; air; look; appearance of the face; favor; good will; kindness
rent Christmas Bells By Henry Wadsworth Longfellow pg.69	a break or breach made by force
incarnate Christmastide By Christina Rossetti pg.71	embodied in flesh; invested in the flesh
ensign Across Delaware By Will Carleton pg.64	a flag or banner; a figured cloth or piece of silk, attached to a staff
malicious December 25, 1914 By Anders Angle pg.72	harboring ill will or enmity; proceeding from extreme hatred or ill will
dale Jack Frost By Gabriel Setoun pg.40	a low place between hills; a vale or valley.

December Vocabulary words, Copy, cut out, fold on the dashed line, and glue together to make flash cards

BLANK VOCABULARY CARDS

Blank Vocabulary ca~d, Copy, cut out, fold on the ddashed line, and glue together to make flash cards

January

"Education must enable one to sift and weigh evidence, to discern the true from the false, the real from the unreal, and the facts from the fiction."
-Martin Luther King Jr.

"since you get more joy out of giving joy to others, You should put a good deal of thought into the happiness that you are able to give."
-Eleanor Roosevelt

"The smallest act of kindness is worth more than the grandest intention."
- Oscar Wilde

"We make a living by what we get, but we make a life by what we give."
-Winston Churchill

The Months
By Sara Coleridge

January brings the snow,
makes our feet and fingers glow.

February brings the rain,
Thaws the frozen lake again.

March brings breezes loud and shrill,
stirs the dancing daffodil.

April brings the primrose sweet,
Scatters daises at our feet.

May brings flocks of pretty lambs,
Skipping by their fleecy damns.

June brings tulips, lilies, roses,
Fills the children's hand with posies.

Hot july brings cooling showers,
Apricots and gillyflowers.

August brings the sheaves of corn,
Then the harvest home is borne.

Warm september brings the fruit,
Sportsmen then begin to shoot.

Fresh October brings the pheasents,
Then to gather nuts is pleasent.

Dull November brings the blast,
Then the leaves are whirling fast.

Chill December brings the sleet,
Blazing fire, and Christmas treat.

---
damns—another spelling of "dam" meaning, a mother of a lamb

The New Year

New Year's Colors
By Kiralee Larsen

BANG!
A brush of pink
Flares against
The starlit night.

BOOM!
A splash of yellow
Sparkles bright
In the dark black.

BAM!
A smudge of blue
Climbs higher
Up to the moon.

BONG!
The strike of twelve
Now begins
A brand-new year.

I Saw Three Ships
By Mother Goose

I saw three ships come sailing by,
Sailing by, sailing by,
I saw three ships come sailing by,
On New Year's Day in the morning.

And what do you think was in them then,
In them then, in them then,
And what do you think was in them then,
On New Year's Day in the morning?

Three pretty girls were in them then,
In them then, in them then,
Three pretty girls were in them then,
On New Year's Day in the morning.

And one could whistle, and one could sing,
The other play on the violin;
Such joy there was at my wedding,
On New Year's Day in the morning.

Resolution
By Michelle Heidenrich Barnes

        Who is to say that
      Tomorrow will be different
     from Today; or that Yesterday
   won't return, a new set of bills in
  hand. I'd like to think I'm better off
for taking time to explore this moment
intimately, savor the spicy-sweet aroma,
  the round ripeness of my tongue, and
   chew no less than twenty-six times:
    once for each regret I may never
     know because time no longer
        swallows me whole

Activity

Shape Poetry Writing Activity

Materials: paper and pencil

Shape poetry is like a fun art project mixed with writing! In shape poetry, the words are arranged to make a shape that looks like the thing you're writing about. For example, if you're writing a poem about a cat, the words might form the shape of a cat!

It's a bit like drawing with words. The way the words are placed on the page helps tell the story and makes the poem even more interesting. So, shape poetry is a cool way to express your ideas and make your words look as fun as they sound!

1. First choose the subject of your poem
2. Choose the shape you would like to write the poem in.
3. Lightly sketch the shape you want your poem to fit in.
4. Write your poem on a separate piece of paper.
5. Now write your poem within the shape you created.

TIPS

-Some of your lines may need irregular spacing. If you look at the arrow you will notice that some words have more than one space between them.

-you can write out your poem by hand, making it easier to adjust the words.

-For younger kids you can print out a pre made shape and let the children write their poem right into the shape.

```
                    I
                  want
               to be the
              best I can be.
             I want to grow up
            and be strong. I want
           to be as smart as I can and
               and  make  sure
                that I am  kind.
                 I want to grow
                 up, I  want to
                 grow up, I want
                 to grow up  like
                 mom  and  dad
```

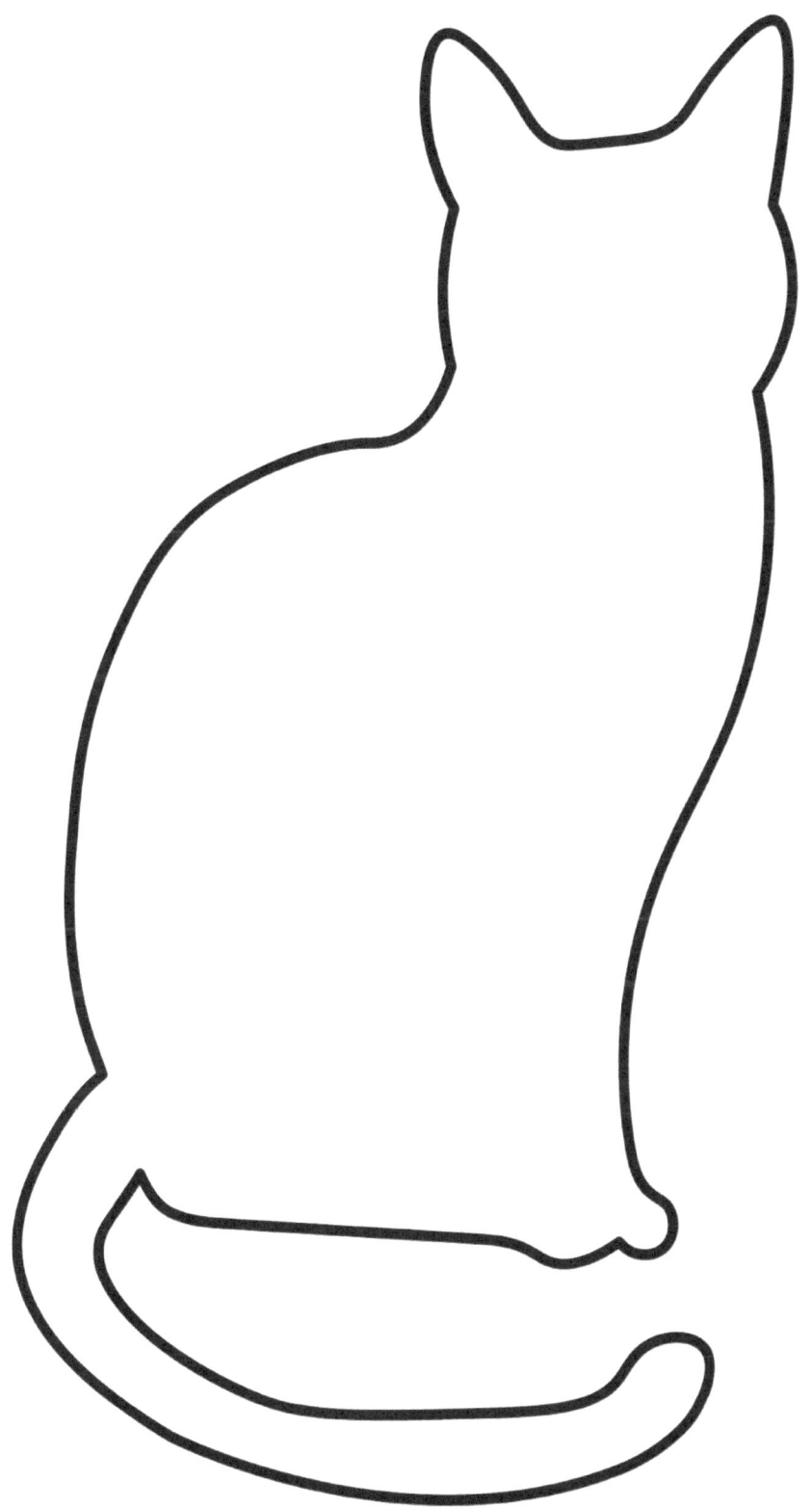

Haiku On Goals
By Christine Owens

A New Year at Last
Excitement, scribing my goals
Cold wind blows outside

---

scribe—to write

May His Life Have Had Purpose
By Christine Owens

He stood for peace and equality
And freedom for all, yes you and me
He walked and walked to make people think
He saw that our country was going to sink
"Darkness cannot drive out darkness" he said
Learned from the bible that his father read

"peace is not merely the absence of tension…
…it is the presence of justice." for all men
"until justice runs down like water" freely
My life will lose all its purpose and meaning.

Winter Fun

If It Were January All The Year
By Annette Wynne

If it were January all the year,
I wonder if I'd like it here,
Finding every place I go—
Snow, snow, always snow!

Snow upon the lane and street,
Snow wherever children meet,
And the houses made of snow,
And the school where children go.

Do you think I'd grow to be
A child quite different from me,
Who'd never seen a thing but snow?
Would I be an Eskimo?

Down We Go
By Christine Owens

I climbed onto my donut
I started sledding down
My dad sitting behind me
Flew down the white ground

The road was getting closer
I don't know what to do
My father bailed
We hit the snow
"Next time I'll just watch you."

Snowball
By Maya Boucha

Do you know just what to do?
When the sky is snowy and blue?
Yes, the best thing of them all
Is make an icy round snowball

Throw them upwards toward the sky
Watch them splatter the ground nearby
You can throw them at your friends
Declare a war that never ends
Make them really big and wide
And soon a snowman friend you'll find

Now you know just what to do
When the sky is snowy and blue
Yes, the best thing of them all
Is make an icy round snowball

Snowball Fight
By Lee Salazar

Sibling Rivalry
Neighborhood
On notice-
War with
Balls of ice
Air born!
Landing
Laughing, Losing..
Fall back to the fort!
Inside make a
Great arsenal of balls-
HAVE
TO WIN!

Activity

Making Snow Tactile Activity

Here is a super fun fake snow you can make at home and you only need two ingredients.

If you want you can give each child their own bowl or container so they can each make their own. Once your snow is made you could have <u>a snowman building contest</u> and give them some beads, strips of felt or flannel and some orange construction paper to get creative with. It will actually have a slightly cool feel to it.

Materials: 2lb box of baking soda, 1-2 cans white shaving cream (like Barbasol soothing aloe), and a bowl or plastic container

Instructions
1. Pour the entire box of baking soda into a plastic container or bowl. If you are wanting to let each kid mix their own then you may want to have more than one box just incase you need more after mixing some.
2. Add some shaving cream and start mixing and kneading it into the baking soda. This part might be a little messy but it will be fun and its easy to clean up.
3. Add more baking soda if the mixture is too wet or add more shaving cream if it is too crumbly.

Indoor Snowball Fight P.E. Activity
If you happen to live in a place where you don't get very much snow, or your snow is just slush, then this is a simple fun way to have a snowball war right inside your home

Materials: socks

1. Collect the socks you have in your drawers (or if you are doing this with a class you can purchase some socks).
2. Roll up two socks together, starting from the toes. Once you get about 4 inches from the top fold the opening of one sock over the

other socks top and around the entire rolled sock. You should be left with a nice tight bundle.
3. Split everyone into teams or everyone can play solo.
4. If you would like you can build forts with fur furniture, pillows, blankets, and more to hide behind.
5. Now have fun having a snowball fight.

Variation

If you want to avoid people throwing "snowballs" at each other then you could set up a few "snow" themed games like knocking over cans decorated as snowmen, tossing the snowballs into big mugs, throwing them into buckets with different amount of points to score.

Wanderlust
By Elizabeth Schroeder

A quiet girl
In a placid room
Gazes out at a world
Subtly lit by the moon

The only sound
Is the whispering breeze
Weaving its way around
Silent, sleeping trees

Sweeping across waves of snow
Seeking a friend who longs to explore
The breeze slithers to and fro
Until it reaches the cottage door

The trees begin to sway
Under the silver moon
As a draft snakes its way
Into the placid room

The draft encircles the girl
Playfully tossing her auburn hair
Teasing her delicate curls
Inviting her to the open air

"Come outdoors," it beckons
"It's so beautiful, you must"
She hesitates only a second,
Then surrenders to wanderlust

With eager anticipation
She greets the crisp winter air
The breeze guides her exploration
To sights of beauty beyond compare

---

placid—serene; mild; unruffled; calm; quiet
subtly— nicely; delicately

The Sugar-Plum Tree
By Eugene Field

Have you ever heard of the Sugar-Plum Tree?
'Tis a marvel of great renown!
It blooms on the shore of the Lollypop sea
In the garden of Shut-Eye Town;
The fruit that it bears is so wondrously sweet
(As those who have tasted it say)
That good little children have only to eat
Of that fruit to be happy next day.

When you've got to the tree, you would have a hard time
To capture the fruit which I sing;
The tree is so tall that no person could climb
To the boughs where the sugar-plums swing!
But up in that tree sits a chocolate cat,
And a gingerbread dog prowls below -
And this is the way you contrive to get at
Those sugar-plums tempting you so:

You say but the word to that gingerbread dog
And he barks with such terrible zest
That the chocolate cat is at once all agog,
As her swelling proportions attest.
And the chocolate cat goes cavorting around
From this leafy limb unto that,
And the sugar-plums tumble, of course, to the ground -
Hurrah for that chocolate cat!

There are marshmallows, gumdrops, and peppermint canes,
With stripings of scarlet or gold,
And you carry away of the treasure that rains,
As much as your apron can hold!
So come, little child, cuddle closer to me
In your dainty white nightcap and gown,
And I'll rock you away to that Sugar-Plum Tree
In the garden of Shut-Eye Town.

---

bough— The branch of a tree; applied to a branch of size, not to a small shoot.
agog— In a state of desire; highly excited by eagerness after an object.
cavorting—jumping or dancing around excitedly; enthusiastically pursuing a disreputable pursuit

Activity

Gingerbread Loaf Cooking Activity
Yields 1 loaf, 4 mini loaves 6+ cupcakes, 24 mini cupcakes
NF

There is nothing like the rich flavor of loaf of Gingerbread. Gingerbread men are cute and all but they can be time consuming. With this loaf you can enjoy the flavor without all of the extra work. If you would like you can even make them into mini loaves or cupcakes. The mini loaves could even be sliced for adorable mini slices.

Ingredients

- ½ cup (104 g)dark brown sugar
- 8 Tbsp butter at room temperature
- ½ cup (236ml) molasses
- 1 ½ tsp vanilla
- 2 large eggs
- 2 cups (240g) flour
- 1 tsp baking soda
- 2 tsp ginger
- ¾ tsp nutmeg
- ½ tsp salt
- 1 cup (236ml) butter milk (or milk with 2 Tbsp lemon juice and left to sit 5 minutes.)
- Powdered sugar (optional)

Instructions
1. Grease a 9X5 inch loaf pan
2. Preheat the oven to 350°F (180°C)
3. In a large mixing bowl cream together the butter and sugar till well combined.
4. Add the molasses, vanilla, and eggs and mix until all mixed in.
5. In a separate mixing bowl mix together the dry ingredients.
6. Using the dry mixture and the buttermilk, alternately add a little of each and mix them in. Do not over mix.
7. Bake
   Single Loaf 45- 50 minutes.
   4 mini loaf pan 25-30 minutes

Cupcakes 15-18 minutes

Mini cupcakes 9-14 minutes (keep an eye on them to not over bake)

8. Cool in the pan for 10 minutes
9. Remove from the pan and finish cooling

Sounds of Their Feet
By Sadie Smith

Spring turns into summer, and summer to fall. Fall then becomes Winter, and winters a brawl.
Young hearts love the snow and as you can see, it is in the harsh weather that their spirits fly free.
Icicles cling, and snowflakes lay. Jack Frost will sing, while Frosty will play.
Step onto the crisp and deep icy paths, and afterward cocoa and warm bubbly baths.
Cheeks all a rosy, and souls lit with fire. Children race out the door in winter attire.
And as the sun lowers from its place in the sky, the children come home with a spark in their eye.
They'll tell you their tales, of igloos and friends. Of slippery step stones and great snowy bends.
The tales will soon end as their eyelids lay low, and the fireplace embers are just barely aglow.
You'll pick up their sleepy little bodies with care, and tuck them in tight with a kiss on their hair.
You'll return to the kitchen to turn out the light, and then lay down your own self to get rest for the night.
Closing your eyes you'll hear winter winds humming, just in time to remember that springtime is coming.
Your kids will soon enough wake the next day, to once again lace up their boots to go play.
Every earthly season of life comes and goes, and with every season a parents heart grows.
These are the moments that make life so sweet, for floors will not always echo with sounds of their feet.

---

brawl— noise; quarrel; scurrility; uproar; to drive or beat away.

Snow
By Mary Mapes Dodge

Little white feathers, filling the air --
Little white feathers! how came ye there?
We came from the cloud-birds sailing so high;
They're shaking their white wings up in the sky.

Little white feathers, how swift you go!
Little white feathers, I love you so!
We are swift because we have work to do;
But hold up your face, and we'll kiss you true.

The Wassail Song
Old Devonshire Carol

Here we come a-wassailing
Among the leaves so green,
Here we come a-wandering
So fair to be seen.

Love and joy come to you
And to your wassail too,
And God bless you, and send you
A happy New Year.

We are not daily beggars
That beg from door to door,
But we are neighbours' children
That you have seen before.

Good Master and good Mistress,
As you sit by the fire,
Pray think of us poor children
Who are wandering in the mire.

Bring us out a table
And spread it with a cloth;
Bring us out a mouldy cheese
And some of your Christmas loaf.

God bless the master of this house,
Likewise the mistress too;
And all the little children
That round the table go.

Activity

Wassail Cooking Activity

Nana Mint, also known as Spearmint, is a type of mint that is often used to make herbal teas. It is known for its refreshing and slightly sweet flavor. The term "Nana" is sometimes associated with a specific type of mint tea popular in the Middle East.

Ingredients for Wassail

- 4 cups apple cider
- 1 cup orange juice
- ¼ cup lemon juice
- 2 cinnamon sticks
- 6 whole cloves or ½ tsp ground cloves
- 1/8 tsp
- 1/8 tsp ground nutmeg

Instructions
1. Combined all ingredients in a large sauce pan or pot.
2. Bring to a simmer
3. Reduce heat to low and continue simmering for 45 minutes to an hour
4. Serve

Variations

There are so many different flavors you can add to your wassail. Try these other additions to create the perfect wassail for your
1 cup pineapple juice
1 orange sliced
1 apple sliced
1 cup cranberries
1 inch fresh ginger sliced
5 allspice berries
2 star anise
1/8 cup brown sugar

Sleigh Bells

The Bells
By Edgar Allen Poe
(part)

Hear the sledges with the bells --
    Silver bells!
What a world of merriment their melody foretells!
   How they tinkle, tinkle, tinkle,
    In the icy air of night!
   While the stars that oversprinkle
   All the heavens, seem to twinkle
    With a crystalline delight;
  Keeping time, time, time,
  In a sort of Runic rhyme,
To the tintinnabulation that so musically wells
 From the bells, bells, bells, bells,
    Bells, bells, bells --
 From the jingling and the tinkling of the bells.

---

merriment— Mirth; gayety with laughter or noise; noisy sports; hilarity; frolick.
crystalline—made of crystals; having a form like a crystal
tintinnabulation—a sound like a bell; a tinkling or ringing sound

Sleigh-Bells
By Mary R.T. McAboy (M.R.M.)

Do you hear the merry bells,
Defiant, wild, and gay?
How their ringing joy dispels
The gloom of life away!

Ringing, dancing, on they come,
Enticing those within--
Tasks and books away therefrom--
With their persuasive din.

"Ding-a-ling, a-ling, a-ling!"
The stars come and and laugh;
"Laugh away!" The sleigh-bells ring,
"We don't do things by half."

See the horses toss their heads,
The snow-balls, —how they fly!
Upward thrown, as each steed treads
The snow, so crisp and dry.

Youthful voices from the sleigh
Commingle with the rhyme;
Sleigh-bells, laughter, speed away,
Enjoy it —now's the time.

Ponies, shake your jetty manes;
My lasses, spend your wit;
Dash away o'er hills and plains,
The queen of night has lit.

---

gay—to be happy
dispel— to scatter by driving or force; to disperse; to dissipate; to banish
entice— to tempt; to incite; to urge or lead astray. To incite or instigate in a good or bad way.
persuasive— having the power of persuading; influencing the mind or passions
comingle— to mix together; mingle in one mass; to blend; mix or unite different substances
jetty— made of jet, or black as jet; to jut; A small pier or projection into a river to narrow & raise water

Jingle Bells
By James Lord Pierpont

Dashing through the snow
In a one-horse open sleigh
O'er the fields we go
Laughing all the way
Bells on bob tail ring
Making spirits bright
What fun it is to ride and sing
A sleighing song tonight!

Jingle bells, jingle bells
Jingle all the way
Oh, what fun it is to ride
 In a one-horse open sleigh,
hey! Jingle bells, jingle bells
Jingle all the way
Oh, what fun it is to ride
 In a one-horse open sleigh!

 A day or two ago,
I thought I'd take a ride
And soon, Miss Fanny
Bright Was seated by my side
The horse was lean and lank
Misfortune seemed his lot
He got into a drifted bank
And then we got upsot

Repeat Stanza Two

 A day or two ago
The story I must tell
I went out on the snow
And on my back I fell
A gent was riding by
In a one-horse open sleigh
He laughed as there I sprawling lie
But quickly drove away

Repeat Stanza Two

Now the ground is white
Go it while you're young
Take the girls tonight
And sing this sleighing song
Just get a bobtailed bay
Two forty as his speed
Hitch him to an open sleigh
And crack! You'll take the lead

Repeat Stanza Two

I'm January
Annette Wynne

I'm January bringing you
A year of days—all brand, brand new;
I step upon the frosty ground.
When chimes and sleighbells ring around;
You welcome me and children sing,
And joy comes into everything.
I bring you love and lots of cheer,
And work and friends for all the year.

Warm Fire

When My Fire Burns Low
By Agnes E. Mitchell

And Old-Time Friends & Twilight Plays,
And Starry Nights, And Sunny Days,
Come Trooping Up The Misty Ways
When My Fire Burns Low.

A Snowman
By Christine Owens
LIMERICK

A snowman sat down by a fire
He felt as if he might expire
He tried to stand up
And slipped on a cup
And now he's a puddle for tires

The Southern Cross Hearth
By Alan Somers

The Bushman jokes, laughs and contemplates
Astride a log with all his mates.

He warms his heart, his toes and socks
The orange glow within a ring of rocks.

Content with life, he knows his place
Among the stars all up in space.

He drifts off to sleep all full of glee
Amazed by viewing his bush TV

---

astride—with one leg on both sides
glee— Joy; merriment; mirth; gayety; particularly, the mirth enjoyed at a feast. A sort of catch or song sung in parts.

I Shiver So Cold
By Henry Mathews
HAIKU

I shiver so cold.
Fire glistens while cold breathes past.
The snowflakes drift by.

My Fire Pit
By Parker Larsen

My fire pit is really bright.
It brings me lots of warmth.
It helps us make good hot dogs.
And something sweet,
Gooey,
Sticky,
And delicious.
These things we call
Marshmallows.

Jack Be Nimble
By Mother Goose

Jack be nimble,
Jack be quick,
Jack jump over the candlestick.

Cold of Snow

Stopping By Woods On A Snowy Evening
By Robert Frost

Whose woods these are I think I know.
His house is in the village though;
He will not see me stopping here
To watch his woods fill up with snow.
My little horse must think it queer
To stop without a farmhouse near
Between the woods and frozen lake
The darkest evening of the year.
He gives his harness bells a shake
To ask if there is some mistake.
The only other sound's the sweep
Of easy wind and downy flake.
The woods are lovely, dark and deep,
But I have promises to keep,
And miles to go before I sleep,
And miles to go before I sleep.

Snow Notes
By Jasmine Ganter
ACROSTIC poem

Soft
Notes
Of
Winter

Winter
By Christina Rossetti

Bread and Milk for breakfast,
   And woolen frocks to wear,
And a crumb for robin redbreast
   On the cold days of the year.

Winter-Time
By Robert Louis Stevenson

Late lies the wintry sun a-bed,
A frosty, fiery sleepy-head;
Blinks but an hour or two; and then,
A blood-red orange, sets again.

Before the stars have left the skies,
At morning in the dark I rise;
And shivering in my nakedness,
By the cold candle, bathe and dress.

Close by the jolly fire I sit
To warm my frozen bones a bit;
Or with a reindeer-sled, explore
The colder countries round the door.

When to go out, my nurse doth wrap
Me in my comforter and cap;
The cold wind burns my face, and blows
Its frosty pepper up my nose.

Black are my steps on silver sod;
Thick blows my frosty breath abroad;
And tree and house, and hill and lake,
Are frosted like a wedding cake.

Winter Grandeur
By Sarah Revo

Often in my darkest hours of heartbreak's bitter woe,
I'm comforted by gentle pow'rs that lie among the snow,

It seems to me there's healing in a silent winter scene,
As snowflakes tumble through the wind and cling to evergreens,

The cooling calm of icy breeze renews my burning heart,
A vast expanse of evening freeze is winter's wondrous art,

My soul is dismal til I see the awe of whitened day,
And whene'er my heart is burdened, sparkling drifts will guide my way,

Crystal frosts and branches flocked allay each care and tear,
For winter's simple beauty is the grandeur of the year.

---

expanse— a spreading; extend; a wide extent of space or body
dismal— dark and gloomy as in a color. Sorrowful; dire; horrid; melancholy; frightful; horrible
allay— to make quiet; to pacify, or appease; to abate, mitigate, subdue or destroy

Winter's Requiem
By Niccole Perrine

Wind is whipping, fierce and strong.
Moonlight hidden all night long.
Clouds billow in the sky
Critters burrow, swiftly shy

Silence steals across the land,
Soft and steady, takes command.
Clouds release their heavy load,
Gently, swiftly down it goes.

Swirling, floating, upon the bowers
Building steadily every hour.
Falling, swirling, bright and clean,
Heavy snow frosts all things seen.

Sun peeks over hill and dale,
Morning light is ever pale.
Tomorrow's come, it's time to play
Night's darkness shifts to sunny day.

Winter Solitude
by Matsuo Basho

Winter solitude –
in a world of one color
the sound of the wind.

January Poetry Writing Prompts

Write about New Years Eve

Write a poem about New Year resolutions

Write a poem about what you think a sleigh ride would be like.

Write a poem about climbing a snowy mountain

Write a poem about Jack frosts birthday

Write a poem about the sound of bells

Write a poem about the best snowball fight ever

Write a poem about building a snowman

Write about poem about kindness

Write a poem about a rabbit jumping though the snow

Write a poem about icicles

Write a poem about ice skating

January Vocabulary Cards

*Download your **FREE**
Vocabulary Flashcards at
<u>www.AYearofPoetryTeaTime.com/shop</u>
And use the code "WINTER" at checkout.*

SELECT JANUARY VOCABULARY

allay Winter Grandeur By Sarah Revo pg.120	to make quiet; to pacify, or appease; to abate; mitigate, subdue or destroy
astride The Southern Cross Hearth By Alan Somers pg.114	with one leg on both sides
dismal Winter Grandeur By Sarah Revo pg.120	dark & gloomy as in a color. sorrowful; dire; horrid; melancholy; frightful; horrible
expanse Winter Grandeur By Sarah Revo pg.120	a spreading; extend; a wide extent of space or body
placid Wanderlust By Elizabeth Schroeder pg.103	serene; mild; unruffled; calm; quiet
dispel Sleigh-Bells By Mary R.T. McAboy pg.111.	to scatter by force; to disperse; to dissipate; to banish

January Vocabulary words, Copy, cut out, fold on the dashed line, and glue together to make flash cards

SELECT JANUARY VOCABULARY

entice Sleigh-Bells By Mary R.T. McAboy pg.111	to tempt; to urge or lead astray. To incite or instigate in a good or bad way.
persuasive Sleigh-Bells By Mary R.T. McAboy pg.111.	having the power of persuading; influencing the mind or passions
comingle Sleigh-Bells By Mary R.T. McAboy pg.111.	to mix together; mingle in one mass; to blend; mix or unite different substances
jetty Sleigh-Bells By Mary R.T. McAboy pg.111	made of jet, or black as jet; to jut; A small pier or projection into a river to narrow & raise water
crystalline Winter Voice By Mala Sabapathy pg.38 The Bells By Edgar Allen Poe pg.110	made of crystals; having a form like a crystal
subtly Wanderlust By Elizabeth Schroeder pg.103	nicely; delicately

January Vocabulary words, Copy, cut out, fold on the dashed line, and glue together to make flash cards

BLANK VOCABULARY CARDS

Blank Vocabulary card, Copy, cut out, fold on the ddashed line, and glue together to make flash cards

February

"I have heard it said that winter, too, will pass, that spring is a sign that summer is due at last. See, all we have to do is hang on."
-Maya Angelou

"Those who are happiest are those who do the most for others."
-Booker T. Washington

"At the end, it's not what you have or even what you've accomplished. It's about who you've lifted up, who you've made better. It's about what you have given back."
-Denzel Washington

"The cumulative impact of thousands of small acts of goodness can be bigger than we imagine."
-Queen Elizabeth

Winter Sleep

Hush, Baby, My Dolly, I Pray You Don't Cry
Nursery Rhyme

Hush, baby, my dolly, I pray you don't cry,
And I'll give you some bread, and some milk by and by,
Or perhaps you like custard, or, maybe, a tart–
Then to either you're welcome, with all my heart

The Sleepy Song
By Josephine Dodge Daskam Bacon

As soon as the fire burns red and low,
And the house up-stairs is still,
She sings me a queer little sleepy song,
Of sheep that go over the hill.

The good little sheep run quick and soft,
Their colors are gray and white;
They follow their leader nose to tail,
For they must be home by night.

And one slips over and one comes next,
And one runs after behind,
The gray one's nose at the white one's tail,
The top of the hill they find.

And when they get to the top of the hill,
They quietly slip away;
But one runs over and one comes next--
Their colors are white and gray.

And over they go, and over they go,
And over the top of the hill,

The good little sheep run quick and soft,
And the house up-stairs is still.

And one slips over and one comes next,
The good little, gray little sheep!
I watch how the fire burns red and low,
And she says that I fall asleep.

Late
By Josephine Preston Peabody

My Father brought somebody up,
  To show us all, asleep.
They came as softly up the stairs
  As you could creep.

They whispered in the doorway there,
  And looked at us awhile.
I had my eyes shut up; but I
  Could feel him smile.

I shut my eyes up close, and lay
  As still as I could keep;
Because I knew he wanted us
  To be asleep.

Cradle Song
by William Blake

Sleep, sleep, beauty bright,
Dreaming in the joys of night;
Sleep, sleep; in thy sleep
Little sorrows sit and weep.

Sweet babe, in they face
Soft desires I can trace,
Secret joys and secret smiles,
Little pretty infant wiles.

As they softest limbs I feel
Smiles as of the morning steal
O'er thy cheek, and o'er thy breast
Where thy little heart doth rest.

O the cunning wiles that creep
In thy little heart asleep!
When thy little heart doth wake,
Then the dreadful night shall break.

Wile— a trick or stratagem practiced for ensnaring or deception; a sly, insidious artifice; to deceive; to beguile.

A Cup Of Tea
By E. L. Sylvester

Phoebe brings the tea-pot, the tea is all a-steam;
Dolly brings the pitcher filled with golden cream.
Rhoda has the dainty cups rimmed about with blue,
And Polly brings the pretty spoons shining bright as new.
The baby trips along behind, looking very droll;
And she, the sweetest of them all, brings the sugar-bowl

Activity

Cambric Tea Making Activity
Have you ever heard of Cambric tea? If you ever read *Little House in the Prairie* or *Ralph Moody's Mary Emma and Company,* you may have come across the main characters talking about their mothers giving them cambric tea. Cambric is actually the name of a cloth that is light and white and that is where the tea gets its name, from its appearance. It was very popular in the 19th and 20th centuries and was given to children or senior citizens who were considered to have a "weak constitution." Children felt very grown-up when given the tea and it would be a treat or sometimes even used to full a not so pacified stomach. It was traditionally made with hot water, milk, sugar, and a splash of tea. Most often it was a black tea but some people would also make it with herbal tea or with spices such as nutmeg, cinnamon, or allspice. In the book Marry Emma and Company the children were served Cambric tea ti warm them after sledding before they were read to and sent off to bed. Below are two ways you can make it. The first one is for herbal tea and the second is for black tea.

Ingredients

- Boiling water
- Milk
- Tea bags of choice
- Sugar
- Spices (optional)

Instructions for Herbal tea
1. Boil a kettle of water
2. Add 3 tea bags of your choice (I used Sleepy Time Tea) to the kettle water and let steep for 5-10 minutes to give it a strong flavor.
3. Fill tea cup ¾ full with tea
4. Add sugar and stir till dissolved
5. Add a 1-2 tablespoons milk

Instructions for black tea
1. Boil water
2. Steep a strong cup of black tea
3. Fill a tea cup ½ full with hot water
4. Add sugar and stir to dissolve
5. Add in milk till it is ¾ full
6. Add 1-2 tablespoons of the black tea

Garnish either cup with some spices if you would like. Freshly grated nutmeg is the best but cinnamon, allspice and ground nutmeg are all good choices

LOVE

My Loves
By Langston Hughes

I love to see the big white moon,
  A-shining in the sky;
I love to see the little stars,
  When the shadow clouds go by.
I love the rain drops falling
  On my roof-top in the night;
I love the soft wind's sighing,
  Before the dawn's gray light.
I love the deepness of the blue,
  In my Lord's heaven above;
But better than all these things I think,
  I love my lady love.

If Love Were Mine
By Annette Wynne

If love were mine, if love were mine,
I know what I would do,
I'd take it, spare it,
Give it, share it,
Lend it, spend it, too.
If beauty I could claim for mine,
To hold, to cherish, too,
I'd strive to spread it,
Pour it, shed it,
Till it flowed the whole world through.
But toil—just common toil—is mine;
And so what I shall do
Is strive to take it,
Carve it, make it,
Into love and beauty, too.

Valentine's Day
By Lillee Larsen
HAIKU

It's such a delight
To get lots of gifts and treats
On Valentine's day.

Cupid's Arrow
By Luke Armstrong

I happily shoot my red winter arrows.
I fire them wide and into the narrows.

I sit in the clouds and watch them fly down,
As they land on loved ones slowly and sound.

Two people who might not otherwise meet,
Now have a chance at love so sweet.

A Red, Red Rose
By Robert Burns

O my Luve is like a red, red rose
   That's newly sprung in June;
O my Luve is like the melody
   That's sweetly played in tune.

So fair art thou, my bonnie lass,
   So deep in luve am I;
And I will luve thee still, my dear,
   Till a' the seas gang dry.

Till a' the seas gang dry, my dear,
   And the rocks melt wi' the sun;
I will love thee still, my dear,
   While the sands o' life shall run.

And fare thee weel, my only luve!
   And fare thee weel awhile!
And I will come again, my luve,
   Though it were ten thousand mile.

Activity

Love Bath Bombs Science Activity

Making your own bath bombs is a fun science lesson and it gets your kids in the bath…what's better than that. The science behind the bath bomb is the same as the all so overdone volcano eruption experiment. Mixing an acid and a base together creates a chemical reaction where protons swap bonds causing CO_2 to be released. The fizz is the gas rising to the surface and escaping from the water. Since the acid and base are in dry form, the water is needed to trigger the reaction. Make these and give them as gifts or you can try out the extra experiments below.

- Heart Molds or any mold of your choice. You can use an ice cube try or halves of Easter Eggs
- 1 cup baking soda
- ½ cup citric acid
- ½ cup cornstarch
- 2 Tbsp coconut oil
- Pink food dye (optional if you want to have a colored bath bomb)
- 3-4 drops essential oils
- Water
-

Other Add ins:
- ¼ cup fine Epson salt
- Pure vanilla powder with any of the following oils: rose, lemon, grapefruit, eucalyptus, lavender, orange, peppermint
- 3 Tbsp activated charcoal
- Lavender blossoms
- dried and ground citrus peel
- 1 tsp ground pumpkin spice

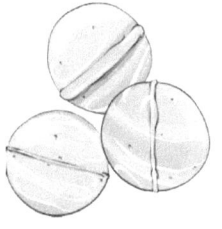

Instructions

1. In a large bowl, combine your citric acid, baking soda, and cornstarch then mix well.
   If you are adding Epson salt mix it in as well
2. Melt your coconut oil and then add a couple of drops of pink food coloring (if your using it) and 3-4 drops essential oil and mix

3. Little by little add your wet mix to the dry mixture and mix quickly every time
4. Once all of your wet mixture is added, your mixture should feel like damp moldable sand.
5. If you are adding in something other than oils then mix them in now.
6. Start filling your chosen mold with your mixture, making sure to press the mixture firmly into the molds. Press it in hard
7. Let dry overnight and carefully remove them from the mold..

The Science explained

In a chemical reaction between citric acid and baking soda, the protons (H^+ ions) play a crucial role. Citric acid is a weak acid, meaning it can donate protons to other substances. Here's how protons are involved in the reaction:

1. **Citric Acid as a Proton Donor:**
   - Citric acid ($C_6H_8O_7C_6H_8O_7$) is a triprotic acid, which means it can donate three protons (H^+ ions) per molecule. In the chemical reaction, citric acid donates protons to the bicarbonate ion ($HCO_3^-HCO_3^-$) present in baking soda.
2. **Baking Soda as a Proton Acceptor:**
   - Baking soda, or sodium bicarbonate ($NaHCO_3NaHCO_3$), acts as a base. It contains the bicarbonate ion ($HCO_3^-HCO_3^-$), which can accept protons. In the reaction, baking soda accepts the protons donated by citric acid.
3. **Formation of Carbon Dioxide Gas:**
   - The transfer of protons from citric acid to baking soda leads to the breakdown of citric acid and the release of carbon dioxide gas (CO_2CO_2). This is the effervescence or fizzing observed during the reaction.
   -

The overall balanced chemical equation for the reaction is:

$C_6H_8O_7$(citric acid)$+3NaHCO_3$(baking soda)$\rightarrow 3CO_2$ (carbon dioxide)$+$
$3H_2O$(water)$+Na_3C_6H_5O_7$(sodium citrate)

Have more fun
Experiment to see if the temperature of the water affects the rate in which the bath bomb dissolves.

Create a table with your children and write down their observations when the bath bomb is placed in ice cold water, tap water, and hot water. Please make sure to be safe and wear safety goggles if you have them. On the left side it could say bath bomb. Across the top it could say ice cold, room temp., and hot or boiling. Record the time it takes for each one to dissolve.

If you have older children/students you could even measure the temperatures of the water. Or take it even another step further and change up the recipe and see what happens when there is more citric acid or more baking soda. Record your findings

Presidents

A Little Boy and a Cherry Tree
By Annette Wynne

A little boy and a cherry tree,
A strong young man who proved to be
A worker with his brain and hand,
A soldier for his well-loved land,
A statesman answering the call
Of home and country, over all,
A glorious patriot, noble son,
A soldier—President—a man!
Was Washington!

Washington
By Annette Wynne

First of our great, we bring
New tributes to your name, and sing
Songs of remembrance on your day;
Years cannot ever wear away
Our thanks to you, nor render less
Our debt for your great worthiness.

Washington's Birthday
By Margaret Elizabeth Sangster

No rockets flamed in sudden fire,
No ringing gladness rocked the spire,
No proud salute, o'er field and town,
Was loud each lesser sound to drown,—
When, on that morning long ago,
A fair young mother, spent and low,
Heard words so sweet: "God give you joy;
The baby is a splendid boy!"

My Childhood Home I See Again
By Abraham Lincoln

My childhood home I see again,
   And sadden with the view;
And still, as memory crowds my brain,
   There's pleasure in it too.

O Memory! Thou midway world
   'Twixt earth and paradise,
Where things decayed and loved ones lost
   In dreamy shadows rise,

And, freed from all that's earthly vile,
   Seem hallowed, pure, and bright,
Like scenes in some enchanted isle
   All bathed in liquid light.

As dusky mountains please the eye
   When twilight chases day;
As bugle-notes that, passing by,
   In distance die away;

As leaving some grand waterfall,
   We, lingering, list its roar—
So memory will hallow all
   We've known, but know no more.

Near twenty years have passed away
   Since here I bid farewell
To woods and fields, and scenes of play,
   And playmates loved so well.

Where many were, but few remain
   Of old familiar things;
But seeing them, to mind again
   The lost and absent brings.

The friends I left that parting day,
   How changed, as time has sped!
Young childhood grown, strong manhood gray,

And half of all are dead.

I hear the loved survivors tell
   How nought from death could save,
Till every sound appears a knell,
   And every spot a grave.

I range the fields with pensive tread,
   And pace the hollow rooms,
And feel (companion of the dead)
   I'm living in the tombs.

Knell—the sound caused by striking a bell; specific to being rung at a funeral; a tolling

pensive—thoughtful; employed in serious study or reflection

The People, Yes
By Carl Sandburg

Lincoln?
He was a mystery in smoke and flags
Saying yes to the smoke, yes to the flags,
Yes to the paradoxes of democracy,
Yes to the hopes of government
Of the people by the people for the people,
No to debauchery of the public mind,
No to personal malice nursed and fed,
Yes to the Constitution when a help,
No to the Constitution when a hindrance
Yes to man as a struggler amid illusions,
Each man fated to answer for himself:
Which of the faiths and illusions of mankind
Must I choose for my own sustaining light
To bring me beyond the present wilderness?

    Lincoln? Was he a poet?
    And did he write verses?
"I have not willingly planted a thorn
    in any man's bosom."
I shall do nothing through malice: what
    I deal with is too vast for malice."

Death was in the air.
So was birth.

Paradox— thoughts or beliefs contrary to popular opinion; seemingly absurd, yet true in fact

debauchery— seduction from duty or allegiance; excess in the pleasures of the table; gluttony

malice— a disposition to injure others without cause, from mere personal gratification or from a spirit of revenge; unprovoked malignity or spite.

Hindrance— impediment; that which stops progression or advance; obstruction

This Dust was Once the Man
By Walt Whitman (about Abraham Lincoln)

THIS dust was once the man,
Gentle, plain, just and resolute, under whose cautious hand,
Against the foulest crime in history known in any land or age,
Was saved the Union of these States.

Snowy Mountain

Fresh Snow
By Christine Owens

Have you ever gone for a walk after a fresh snow
So clean and white

No trace of anyone ever being there
No one in sight

Silence is all you can hear
Like there's a blanket over your ears

Imagine there only being you
The world starting anew

Your body washed over with a sense of still
With peace you fill

Blizzard Hike
By Luca Rullo

I took a hike over a hill
In the cold winter chill
My boots crunched down below
They crunched the hard, icy snow

I stopped and looked at the heaps of white
No green, no blue, not in my sight
What a winter wonderland I've found!
It is so quiet; I hear no sound

I feel peaceful and I feel calm
 I turn over my hands and open my palms
I thank the Lord for this snowy day
With a cold breeze and sunshine rays

The Peak
By Hannah Seaman

Choosing to climb Everest,
Lovely idea, right?
Incredible views,
Marvelous height.
But is it what it seems?
Icicles, crevasses,
Nasty snowy winds.
Grey skies loom above.

Engulfed in a snowstorm,
Vicious winds hit your face, you
Even lose a glove.
Reaching the top,
Exquisite, you can't even speak
So was it worth it,
To climb to the peak?

Crevasse—a deep open crack, typically in a glacier or in the ground
loom—above the surface either of sea or land; a goose sized bird; wood device for weaving cloth
engulfed—surround or cover completely
exquisite— nice; exact; very excellent; complete; being in the highest degree; extreme

Yeti
By Micah Seaman

A big hairy Yeti at the top of Mount Everest, having a good old feast.

Except he's not very happy cause they think of him as a beast.

He sometimes wishes he was bold enough to meet the people out there,

Because he thinks they would really like his thick and fluffy hair.

Every year Mount Everest grows taller,

And every year his hope grows smaller.

He thinks of himself as his cave; cold, empty and alone.

All he wants from the bottom of his heart is a friend to call his own.

A Winter's Tale
by D. H. Lawrence

Yesterday the fields were only grey with scattered snow,
And now the longest grass-leaves hardly emerge;
Yet her deep footsteps mark the snow, and go
On towards the pines at the hills' white verge.

I cannot see her, since the mist's white scarf
Obscures the dark wood and the dull orange sky;
But she's waiting, I know, impatient and cold, half
Sobs struggling into her frosty sigh.

Why does she come so promptly, when she must know
That she's only the nearer to the inevitable farewell;
The hill'Is steep, on the snow my steps are slow -
Why does she come, when she knows what I have to tell?

Verge—to tend downwards; to bend; to slope; a rod or staff carried by one in authority

obscure— to hide from the view; not easily understood; to conceal; to make unknown

An Arrogant Journey Of A River
By Julliet Hiller

Fairly, fairly, I ripple over the rocks.
Nothing, nothing can stop my journey down.
The deer will sip, the birds peck, the wolves will lap.
Still I slip and slide to where an ocean is found.

Crispy, cold I wash the roots of the mountains.
Coming changes with leafless trees and gray ground.
The deer are slow, the birds; flown, the wolves are gaunt.
Still I slip and slide to where an ocean is found.

Heavy, heavy the jagged parts I carry.
Slowly, slowly the frozen pieces are bound.
My rush is not, my flow is froze, my pride; gone.
Still, I wait in the riverbed until found.

Gaunt— lean and haggard because of suffering from hunger, or age; grim in appearance

Winter Trees
By Annalise Fellows

Stark and bare
Against the sky.
Reaching up
So very high.
Standing there,
So very cold.
They look so fragile —
So very old.

Sledding
By Cristabella Salazar

Sleighing
Laying on my back
Eyes closed tight
Donut sled held tight
Dips and bumps
IN THE AIR!
Not on the
Ground!?

Activity

Acrostic Poetry Writing Activity

Materials: paper and pencil

Acrostic poetry is a playful way to write poems! In an acrostic poem, you pick a word, and each letter of that word becomes the start of a line in your poem. When you read those lines from top to bottom, they spell out the word you chose!

For example, if you want to write about "SUN," each line of your poem might start with a word or phrase that begins with the letters S, U, and N. It's a cool way to make a poem and have fun with words at the same time!

TIP
If writing a full sentence is difficult for any of your children or students then you can come up with a single word for each letter. For instance if the word is BIRD then the words could be

Beautiful
Intelligent
Resilient
Dove

If you wanted to use the same word with sentences it could look like this.

Beautiful elegant bird of the world
Interested in crumbs on the ground
Ready to fly any moment to safety
Dodging feet and wheels to survive

How to choose your word to start with

- Use the first name of a person, a book character, relative, author, friend...
- Use your full name
- A word related to a special event like wedding, child birth, graduation, surgery...
- A new word you have learned like erode, emulsify, mobius, eclectic...
- A type of animal like lion, dog, elephant, cheetah, otter, mouse, rat, oxalate...

GIVE IT A TRY, HAVE FUN WITH IT!

Winter Animals

Sing, Little Bird
By Mother Goose

Sing, little bird,
   When the skies are blue;
Sing, for the world
   Has need of you;
Sing when the skies
   Are overcast;
Sing when the rain
   Is falling fast

Sing, happy heart
   When the sun is warm;
Sing in the winter's
   Coolest storm;
Sing little songs,
   O heart so true;
Sing, for the world
   Has need of you.

Pine Warbler Thanks
By Sharon Dodd

There she is!
I've got to go tell her!

I perch on a twig
In the dormant Crepe Myrtle she's trimming,
And look at her with a grateful glisten in my eye.

She puts her work on freeze
And tenderly eyes me.
I hop closer, my yellow belly full
Of sweet sunflower seeds
And take a deep breath . . .
thankyouthankyouthankyouthankyouthankyou
I gurgle with blessed bliss.

She smiles,
And I know
That she knows
How delighted I am
That she hung the winter bird feeder.

Groundhog
By Christine Owens

The noble groundhog peeks out of his hill
Will we see Spring or endure winter still?

Endure— To last; to continue the same without perishing; to remain; to bear without yielding

Shelter
By Alex Van Komen

There is the hen with wings of gold
Who stood all night out in the cold,
With beady eyes and down of lace,
And dainty step so full of grace.
She lost her way that icy night,
In mounds of snow with frosty bite.
She found a place without the storm
And tucked her head to keep it warm.
She stayed that way 'till day had come
And snow resided from the sun.
She raised her head from silent sleep
And sorted out her bundled heep.
She cocked her head and looked around
Then picked herself up from the ground.
She found her way back to the flock,
Wherein she found her little cock.
He crowed this tale out bright and true.
And on and on this story flew.
We look upon this hero bold,
This little hen out in the cold.
With wings of gold and beady eyes,
The greatest comes in little size.

Cocked—tilted in a particular direction
cock—a rooster

Penguins
By Alex Somers
HAIKU

Penguins are so nice
Playing in the water and
Sliding on the ice.

Winter Wolf
By Spencer Van Komen

Hunter of the night,
With fangs of white.

Pray you softly stalk,
In a swift walk.

Your prints in the snow,
They seem to glow.

Your fur dark as night,
Stops the cold's bite.

Snow falls on your nose,
As the wind blows.

Your crown of glory,
Holds your story.

Oh mighty wolf true,
Just look at you.

Stalk—walk behind something undetected; the stem of a plant; walk with high and proud steps

Chinese New Year

Chinese New Year
By Wang Anshi

The old year has passed in the sound of firecrackers, and the Tusu wine is enjoyed with a warm spring breeze.

The rising sun shines on thousands of households, and the old peach symbols are removed and replaced with new peach symbols.

What Will The New Year Bring
By Cui Tu ca. 854 AD
Chinese New Year

The road to Ba is a long, long way
Still, I make this perilous journey of ten thousand li
In the melting snow beneath jagged mountains at night
A stranger in a strange land

Alone, gradually growing distant from family and friends
And closer instead to my companions
How does one bear moving from place to place,
What will the New Year bring?

Poem On Selling Silliness
By Fan Chengda

《甲午元旦》
萧疏白髮不盈颠，守岁围炉竟废眠。
剪烛催乾消夜酒，倾囊分遍买春钱。
听烧爆竹童心在，看抉桃符老兴偏。
鼓角梅花添一部，五更欢笑拜新年。

Despite thinning white hair,
I stayed up for a night to feast on New Year's Eve.
The burning candle urges me to drink up;
I emptied my pocket, giving children coins for good luck.
Hearing the noise of firecrackers, I'm cheerful like a child;
Seeing new spring couplets hang, I sense closure of the old year.
Listening to the "Plum Blossom" tune one more time;
Soon, the day breaks and people greet one another with laughter.

New Years Eve
By Wen Zhengming

《除夕》
人家除夕正忙时，我自挑灯拣旧诗。
莫笑书生太迂腐，一年功事是文词。

Others are busy celebrating the New Year,
But I'm sorting old poems under the lamp.
Don't laugh at me for being pedantic;
My most important achievements of the year are poems and prose.

Stay Up Late On New Years Eve
By Su Shi (aka SUDongpo)

《守岁》
欲知垂尽岁，有似赴壑蛇。
修鳞半已没，去意谁能遮。
况欲系其尾，虽勤知奈何。
儿童强不睡，相守夜欢哗。
晨鸡且勿唱，更鼓畏添挝。
坐久灯烬落，起看北斗斜。
明年岂无年，心事恐蹉跎。
努力尽今夕，少年犹可夸。

The old year is parting,
Like a snake slithering into a deep ravine.
Scales barely seen; none could stop its course.
Try as hard as we might to grab its tail, but in vain.
Children strive to stay awake, laugh and play all night long.
Rooster, please don't crow yet, but the morning drum is urging.
The lamp has burnt out, and the Big Dipper descends on the horizon.
Year after year, time flies and my worries are futile.
Better to cherish this night, and I still have the spirit of a young man.

New Years Day
By Wang Anshi

《元日》
爆竹声中一岁除，春风送暖入屠苏。
千门万户曈曈日，总把新桃换旧符。

With the noise of firecrackers, the old year has passed away;
The spring breeze has infused warmth in the Tusu wine.
When the rising sun shines on the doors of each household,
New peach wood charms are put up to replace the old.

Snow on New Year's Eve
By Lu You
Chinese New Year

《除夜雪》
北风吹雪四更初，嘉瑞天教及岁除。
半盏屠苏犹未举，灯前小草写桃符。

In early morning, a north wind brings snow;
It's a blessing from Heaven arriving in time.
I haven't yet raised my half cup of Tusu wine to toast the New Year;
Busy writing peach wood charms by lamplight.

Activity

Chinese Almond Cookies Cooking Activity
Yields 1 loaf, 4 mini loaves 6+ cupcakes, 24 mini cupcakes

Almonds have positive symbolism in Chinese culture, representing good fortune and prosperity. Including almonds in cookies may have been a way to infuse these positive connotations into the treat. The Chinese almond cookie has a history that intertwines with Chinese-American culinary traditions. While the exact origin is not definitively documented, it is believed to have originated in the United States by immigrants of Chinese heritage. They are popular during Chinese New Year because they are viewed to represent a coin which are symbols of good fortune. This recipe does need time to chill in the fridge for 2 hours so make sure to leave time for that.

Ingredients

- 1 1/3 cup (149 g) lightly packed almond flour
- 1 cup (227 g) butter at room temperature.
- Pinch of salt
- 2 eggs
- 1 tsp almond extract
- 1 ¾ cup (219 g) flour
- 1 cup (200 g) plus an additional tablespoons sugar
- ½ tsp baking soda
- Sliced almonds or blanched almonds
- 1 Tbsp water

Instructions
1. Beat together the butter and sugar until light and fluffy.
2. Mix in the almond flour, 1 egg and almond extract until it is well incorporated.
3. Whisk together the dry ingredients and then add it to the Almond mixture until combined.
4. Place a piece of plastic wrap out on the counter and put the cookie dough onto it. Flatten it out a little and cover with the plastic wrap and chill for 2 hours.

5. Preheat your oven to 325° (163°C) and put parchment paper on the sheet.
6. Roll the dough into 1-inch balls. Place on cookie sheet leaving at least 1 inch space and flatten the ball with the palm of your hand.
7. Whisk the second egg with the Tbsp of water and brush the top of each cookie with the egg wash.
8. adorn each cookie with a gently pressed almond while the wash is still wet.
9. Bake for 15-17 minutes or until the top becomes a golden brown.
10. Let cool on the sheet for 5 minutes before removing to a cookie rack to finish cooling.

Winters End

Frost
By Ella Gray

The Frost
Upon the ground there lies a frost,
A cold and stinging blight,
And all of green and growing thing
Is hidden, choked, and lost.
The sun is white, and hard, and dead,
And warms not any thing;
The wind blows harsh across the snow
And wails a tale of dread.
But though the time seems stopped in gloom,
Congealed in dismal chill,
This time will pass—this austere plain
Will boast a field of blooms.
For all its grief,
The world goes on—
The frost
        Must always
            Melt.
Upon my heart there lay a frost,
A cold, and stinging blight
And every good and wholesome thing
Seemed hidden, choked, and lost.
My eyes were cold, and hard, and dead,
And saw not anything
Of beauty, and a bitter pall
Seemed wrapped about my head.
And thus my heart would lie—but then
You came and spoke of spring.
You thawed the heart too long too cold,
And made it warm again.
You cheered my grief,
You taught me this—
The frost
        Must always
            Melt.

Blight— any thing nipping or blasting; a disease that affects a plant; to frustrate

My Souls Winter
By Ericka Harris

"Winter begins beautifully—
Fluffy snowflakes settle on barren trees.
Weeks pass on, flurries turn to blizzards.
White blankets the ground in a chilling embrace.
Snowdrifts accumulate.
Leafless branches deflect near breaking.
Not quite how I wished this winter would be.
Will this season ever end?
The snow plow gives temporary relief;
Still, piles of icy compacted graupel amass.

It's been lifeless too long for my liking.
I look around, beauty is buried.
Motionless. Lingering. Stagnant.
External reminders that life is hard.
How long, Creator, will this season last?

Creator of all seasons,
Tend to the soil that is my soul.
Autumn sown seeds hibernate.
My winter faith unfolds underground,
Unable to understand the deep root development.
Silent. Cold. Seemingly still.

Wait for it, my soul, spring is coming.
I hope in the Maker of the seasons.
Make known to me Your companionship while waiting.
I remember Your daffodils in the spring,
Your sunshine of the summer,
Your harvest of the autumn seasons past.

Brilliant blue buds of the forget-me-not flower
Springing forth—
Hope."

Barren—bleak and lifeless or an animal or human who cannot produce offspring.
Graupel—softer than hail, it is a snow that has melted, then flash cooled, forming soft ice pellets
stagnant—motionless; still; not agitated; not active, often referring to water or a person's life

An English Winter
By Lilian Crisp

Crystalized jewels of water hang from the branches of an oak,
Flakes of fine, white powder, fall across the frosty ground,
Whilst the silver blade of an axe steals the last breath of the mature pine.

The rich scent of winter fills the air,
As spices blend,
Ginger, nutmeg, cinnamon, and cloves.

Warm woollen mittens,
Granny Mavis' knitted bobble hat,
Families warmly embrace.

Fire flickering, licking the chill,
Drinking hot cocoa,
With marshmallows to toast.

And even before winter is over,
The first blooms of crocuses show their dainty, white buds,
And we know, winter is easing.

But not for long,
For after three seasons,
We will encounter winter once more.

The Fairies' Nook in Winter
By Rhylin Taylor

The oak so full of life in Spring
Was still quite pretty, though not green
Icicles hung on every bough
Branches white were barren now.

The forest sprites began to plot
They liked their seasons nice and hot
They did not like this frozen age
How could they drive the frost away?

So then the imps began to pelt
The World with joy, so they could melt
This cold and cheerless icy clime
And laugh away the wintertime.

Bough— The branch of a tree; applied to a branch of size, not to a small shoot.

Barren—bleak and lifeless or an animal or human who cannot produce offspring.

February Poetry Writing Prompts

Write about love

Write a poem about Valentin's Day

Write a poem about cupid

Write a poem about someone you love

Write a poem about George Washington

Write an Acrostic poem with Abraham Lincolns name

Write a poem about Chinese New Year

Write an Acrostic poem using your name

Write a poem about a groundhog

Write a poem A melting snowman

Write a poem about crocus flowers growing in the snow

Write a poem about nature

February Vocabulary Cards

*Download your **FREE**
Vocabulary Flashcards at
<u>www.AYearofPoetryTeaTime.com/shop</u>
And use the code "WINTER" at checkout.*

SELECT FEBRUARY VOCABULARY

barren My Souls Winter By Ericka Harris pg.167 The Fairies' Nook in Winter By Rhylin Taylor pg.169	bleak and lifeless; an animal or human who cannot produce offspring.
blight Frost By Ella Gray pg.166	any thing nipping or blasting; a disease that affects a plant; to frustrate
debauchery The People, Yes By Carl Sandburg pg.147	seduction from duty or allegiance; excess in the pleasures of the table; gluttony
gaunt An Arrogant Journey Of A River By Julliet Hiller pg.152	lean and haggard because of suffering from hunger, or age; grim in appearance
graupel My Souls Winter By Ericka Harris pg.167	softer than hail, it is snow that has melted, then flash cooled, forming soft ice pellets
hindrance The People, Yes By Carl Sandburg pg.147	impediment; that which stops progression or advance; obstruction

February Vocabulary words, Copy, cut out, fold on the dashed line, and glue together to make flash cards

SELECT FEBRUARY VOCABULARY

knell My Childhood Home I See Again By Abraham Lincoln pg.145	the sound caused by striking a bell; specific to being rung at a funeral; a tolling
obscure A Winter's Tale By D. H. Lawrence pg.152	to hide from the view; not easily understood; to conceal; to make unknown
paradox The People, Yes By Carl Sandburg pg.147	thoughts or beliefs contrary to popular opinion; seemingly absurd, yet true in fact
pensive My Childhood Home I See Again By Abraham Lincoln pg.145	thoughtful; employed in serious study or reflection
verge A Winter's Tale By D. H. Lawrence pg.152	to tend downwards; to bend; to slope; a rod or staff carried by one with authority
stagnant My Souls Winter By Ericka Harris pg.167	motionless; still; not agitated; not active, often referring to water or a person's life

February Vocabulary words, Copy, cut out, fold on the dashed line, and glue together to make flash cards

BLANK VOCABULARY CARDS

Blank Vocabulary card, Copy, cut out, fold on the ddashed line, and glue together to make flash cards

Mini Poet Biographies

Ableson, Alter — 1880-1964 — New York, USA
Ableson grew up in Manhattan, New York and was born to Lithuanian parents. He studied classic poets such as Keats, Shakespeare, Milton and Shelley. In 1903 he received his Masters in Hebrew Liturature. He served as a Rabbi in synagogues in New York, Rhode Island, and New Jersey. His first collection of poetry published was Sambatyon and Other Poems in 1931. He also translated the works of Hebrew poets Halevi and Chaim Nachman Bialik.

Alcott, Louisa May — 1832-1888 — Massachusetts, USA
Alcott was born in Germantown, Pennsylvania, into a family of transcendentalist thinkers. She grew up around prominent writers and thinkers, including Henry David Thoreau and Ralph Waldo Emerson.
Alcott's family faced financial struggles, and she took on various jobs as a teacher, governess, and seamstress to support them. Alcott was best known as the author of *Little Women* and *Little Men*, and wrote several sequels to including *Little Men* and *Jo's Boys*. Alcott also wrote short stories, thrillers, and poetry. She was a nurse during the Civil War for six weeks. Throughout her life, Alcott advocated for women's rights, women's suffrage, and the abolition of slavery. Her first publication was *Flower Fable* in 1854.

Agle, Anders — b. 2006 — California, USA
Agle's poetry is inspired by great events in history and his innermost thoughts, desires, and feelings. IHe is one of five brothers and he is inspired by his older brother, Soren, who writes music. Agle loves playing football, learning new and interesting things while studying English and History, reading fantasy fiction and LDS romance novels, eating good seafood, hanging out with friends, and sleeping.

Armstrong, Luke — b. 2012 — Maryland, USA
Armstrong was born in Prince Frederick MD. He currently resides in Maple Valley WA with his parents Dean and Carolyn Armstrong, younger brother Liam and rescue cat Ellie. Armstrong was 10 years old when he wrote his poem "Under the Sea." He enjoys writing poetry because "it allows me to express myself in my own way to the world." Some of his favorite books are currently the Warrior Cat series, all the Narnia book series, Greek mythology and Minecraft Dungeon series. Some of his academic awards he has achieved have included the gold level on the ETC National Greek Exam and he is also a Catholic Schoolhouse Super Scholar Award Winner in several subject areas. Armstrong plays outdoor premier level soccer year-round and enjoys all things soccer. Other interests and pass times include snowboarding, playing piano and recorder, playing pickle-ball and video games.

Barnes, Michelle Heidenrich — b. 1967 — Florida, USA
Barnes is a children's poet and anthologist from Florida. Growing up she enjoyed the performing arts, music and dance. She loved how they could tell stories. She has lived in New York, Massachusetts, New Mexico, and Australia. She was a finalist for Alachua County Poet Laureate, she has poems in several anthologies, including *A World of Poems*, *Imperfect: poems about mistakes, I Am Someone Else, The Poetry of US, One Minute Till Bedtime,* and *For Every Little Thing*. Her *The Best of Today's Little Ditty* series offers poetry practice for writers of all ages and abilities.

Blake, William — 1754-1827 — England
Blake was born in Soho, London. He grew up to be an English poet, printmaker, and painter. He attended school long enough to learn to read and write. After that, he learned at home, read books of his choosing, and at this point he became interested in poetry. He attended a drawing school at age ten. He was also a great artist in his time and was proclaimed by Johnathan Jones to be "far and away the greatest artist Britain has ever produced." Blake was considered idealistic and a bit mad for his views on politics and religion.

Boucha, Maya, —b. 2010 — Utah, USA

Boucha has been homeschooled for 7 years, and she enjoys studying photography and piano. She also enjoys taking care of her chickens. Boucha has travelled to 17 US states and loves to travel. She was published in *A Poetry Tea Time Adventure* in 2023. She likes reading any poem that has an interesting story and fun rhymes.

Brémont, Anna de — 1849-1922 — New York, USA

Brémont was born in New York City but after her father passed away her mother moved them to Cincinnati, Ohio. She became an journalist, poet, singer, and novelist. Her first collection of poems, Love Poems, was published in 1889. She was well known for a set of collections titled The World of Music published in 1892. She did a poetry and musical tour through Australia, and South Africa and also traveled to Europe and the UK.

Brontë, Emily — 1818-1848 — England

Brontë was the third child of the Brontë children after her brother Patrick Branwell Brontë. She grew up to be a poet and novelist, best known for her novel *Wuthering Heights*. She also collaborated with her sisters in publishing a book *Poems under the pen names* Currer, Ellis, and Acton Bell, her pen name being Ellis Bell. People found her poetry to be "poetic genius." The sisters grew up in Haworth, England.

Burns, Robert — 1759-1796 — Scotland
Burns was born in Alloway, Scotland in a house that was built by his father. William Burnes (his father) was a tenant farmer and his mother, Agnes Broun, was the daughter of a tenant farmer. He was the eldest of seven children. When he was seven his family moved to the Mount Oliphant farm where his father did the same work. Burns grew up doing manual farm labor and in poverty.
He had very little formal education and gained most of his learning from his father. His father taught all of his children math, geography, history, reading, writing, and even wrote a *A Manual of Christian Beliefs*. He did attend an "adventure school" where he learned some Latin and French from John Murdock and later spent three weeks living with Murdock to study Latin, French and grammar more in depth. At age fifteen he was the main laborer at the farm and he met Nelly Kilpatrick who introduced him to poetry. His first attempt at a poem was "O, Once I Lov'd A Bonnie Lass." He became a poet and lyricist who wrote in both English and Scots dialect. Burns is still very popular in Scotland, and in 2009, a public vote won him the title of "Greatest Scot" He was a collector of folk songs. His poem turned song "Auld Lang Syne" is popular around the world.

Canton, William —1845-1926 — England
Canton was born in China to a Catholic family and he spent most of his childhood in Jamaica. He became a teacher and writer. He worked in both England and Scotland. When his daughter passed away at age 10 he was hear broken and took on a job to write the history of the Bible Society, a task that took him five years. After that he dedicated his writing to children's literature. His works spaned poetry, essays, and novels.

Carleton, Will —1845–1912 — Michigan, USA
Carleton was an American poet best known for his poetry that captured rural life and social issues in the late 19th century. Born in Michigan, Carleton's work often depicted the struggles and joys of everyday people in the American Midwest. His most famous poem is 'Over the Hill to the Poor-House'. Carleton's writing, characterized by its sentimental and moralistic tone, resonated with a broad audience and contributed to the popularization of poetry during his time. His work provides a snapshot of the social and cultural landscape of the post-Civil War era.

Coleridge, Coleridge — 1802-1852 — England
Coleridge was was born in Keswick, English. She grew up to be an author and poet, and she is the daughter of the famous poet Samuel Taylor Coleridge. She was well educated and her first work of was translating works that were in Latin in ancient French. Her first publication was inspired by her own children, *Pretty Lessons in Verse for Good Children* in 1834. Coleridge wrote poetry, essays, and literary criticism, and she played a significant role in preserving and editing her father's works, contributing to the understanding of the Coleridgean literary legacy. Her own poetic works often reflected a blend of Romantic ideals and Victorian sensibilities. One of her most popular poems was "The Months" which is included in this publication. Her longest publication came out in 1837. It was a story that she originally started for her son titled Phantasmion, A Fairy Tale.

Crisp Lilian — b. 2012 — Australia
Crisp is homeschooled, freeing up lots of time for her to do things she enjoys. She fills her time with singing, baking and writing poetry. She loves to look out the window and daydream. She writes her emotions down and loves the rhythm and flow of writing. Her grandma, in England, is said to be a bit of a poet growing up!

Cui Tu — 854-883 — China
Cui Tu was a Chinese poet during the late Tang Dynasty. Known for his elegant and melancholic poetry, Cui Tu's work often explored themes of nature, beauty, and the fleeting nature of life. He was associated with the "Jian'an" poetic style, characterized by its simplicity and restraint. Despite his relatively short life, Cui Tu left a lasting impact on Chinese poetry, influencing later generations with his graceful verses that expressed a deep sensitivity to the human experience.

De La Mare, Walter — 1873-1956 — England
De La Mare received his education at the St. Paul's Cathedral School. His maternal grandfather, Dr. Colin Arrott Browning, was a naval surgeon and author. De La Mare didn't like his name and asked people to call him Jack. He believed that there were two types of imagination. He was known to say "children are, in short, visionaries." He said that a child's thoughts are full of both creativity and ingenuity. But the more exposure they have to the world the more their imagination fades away. Worked for 18 years doing statistics for an oil company. Sir Henry Newbolt provided a way for him to live on a Civil List pension so he could focus on writing. He is best known for his writings for children and his poem *The Listeners*. He also published *Collected Stories for Children* with 17 original fantasy fairy tales in 1947.

Dodd, Sharon — b. 1962 — Texas, USA
Dodd was born Sharon Sipps Dodd and is an author, educator, and poet. Dodd is a devout Catholic and draws her inspiration from her daily studies of the gospel and crafting words to honor those embraces. She writes with the hope that her readers will be inspired to pause a little and recognize the Creator's glorious Spirit in the world around them. Dodd wrote her first poem at age 18 and uses the pen name Rose of Sharon. Her first published collection of poetry is *Offerings* was published in 2021. She was also a winner of the Catholic Kidlit Writing contest in 2021 for her poem "The King". You can explore more of Dodd's work at RoseOfSharon.net

Dodge, Mary Mapes — 1831-1905 — New York, USA

Even though Dodge's father, James Jay Mapes, was a professor, her and her siblings were all educated at home by a governess and tutors. Not only was she educated in English, she was also versed in French, Latin, music, drawing and showed talent in many areas. In 1859 she did a publication project with her father. She did a number of editing and publishing projects over her life time, one of which was *Rhymes and Jingles* in 1874.

Fan Chengda — 1126-1193 — China
Fan Chengda was a Chinese poet, writer, and government official during the Southern Song Dynasty. Renowned for his travel writings, he is best known for the work "On the World," which chronicles his extensive journeys and observations. In addition to his travelogue, Fan Chengda wrote poetry that often celebrated the natural world and conveyed a sense of nostalgia. His literary contributions and official service reflected a deep engagement with both the cultural and political aspects of his time, making him a notable figure in Chinese history.

Faustino, Jeremiah — b. 2012 — Illinois, USA
Faustino was born in the Philippines and later his family move to the United States. He developed a rich vocabulary through reading books. He is creative and loves crafting various toys (such as board games and card games) and writing short stories, picture books and graphic novels for the sole entertainment of his family and especially his younger brothers.

Fellows, Anneliese — b. 2008 — Michigan, USA
Fellows was born in Ann Arbor, Michigan the oldest of two children. She is fascinated with her four pet rats and adores bats. She loves to write poetry and fantasy sci-fi stories. She is currently working on a novel titled *The Strange Adventures of Pangolin*. When she isn't writing she does enjoy running and does it competitively in Cross Country. She is a Christian and feels revived and basked in Gods glory when writing her poetry.

Field, Eugene – 1850–1895 – Missouri, USA
Field was a journalist and poet. He was known for his humorous writing and children's poetry. He first started publishing his poetry in 1879 with his poem "Christmas treasures." His most famous children's poem is "Wynken, Blynken, and Nod."

Frost, Robert – 1874–1963 – Massachusetts, USA
Frost was born in San Francisco, California, but moved after his father's death. His first poem was published in his high school's magazine. He did many kinds of jobs as an adult, but felt his true calling was poetry. He sold his first poem: "My Butterfly. An Elegy." His first book of poetry was published in England in 1913 titled *A Boy's Will*. He won many Pulitzer Prizes and was presented with the Congressional Gold Medal. He was known for his ability to use American Colloquialism and capturing rural life.

Ganter, Jasmine —b. 1990 — Massachusetts, USA
Ganter was born in Massachusetts and currently resides there as and proud mother of four children. She home educates her children and enjoys putting pen to paper to write stories. Ganter is also a lover of books. Her first publication was "Basilisk Bested" in Gnomes and Ungnomes: Poems of Hidden Creatures (Writers Loft Press, Nov2023).

Gray, Ella — b. 2006 — Tennessee, USA
Gray was born and raised in Tennessee and has grown up with a love for music and literature. She finds inspiration for her poetry in nature, the trials and joys of life, and the humor of interpersonal relationships. She loves her family, her church, sewing and knitting, but mostly, her dog Puck.

Harris, Ericka — b. 1973 — Oregon
Harris's regular exposure to poetry began while living cross culturally and home educated her children. Her family enjoys traveling and tasting all the yummy cultural foods available. Professionally, she teaches Christian leaders about loss(es) and provides a space for processing their own grief. Harris's personal laments inspired the poem "My Soul's Winter." Harris wrote a creative memory journal called "Remembering" – follow its creative prompts to reminisce and honor a friend or family member; release coming soon.

Hepburn, Thomas Nicoll — 1861-1930 — Scotland
Hepburn grew up to be a poet and an author. He used the pseudonym, Gabriel Setoun. Some of his most popular poems are 'Jack Frost', 'Romance', and 'The World's Music'.

Hiller, Julliette — b. 1983 — California, USA
Hiller grew up on the west coast of the United States; California, Arizona, and Washington state where she currently lives with her husband and seven children. After college, and taking a gap year in Scotland, Hiller served in the United States Army as a medic. She and her husband have fostered several children from Ukraine, and they have recently adopted two sisters from Africa. Hiller is passionate about homeschooling her children, loving Jesus, leading worship at church, teaching ballet, and, of course, writing.

Hughs, Langston — 1901-1967 — Kansas, USA
Hughs was raised by his grandmother after his father left and his mother travelled to find work. His was raised to have pride in his African American heritage. His childhood was very lonely growing up with his grandmother until he started to read books. In his autobiography *The Big Sea* he said "I began to believe in nothing but books." After his grandmother passed away, he lived with his mother in Lincoln Illinois. Here, in grammar school, he was chosen to be the class poet. By high school they had moved to Cleveland, Ohio. Here his literary activity increased and he wrote for his school newspaper, wrote poetry, short stories and his first jazz poem titled *When Sue Wears Red."* His first publication was in 1921 in *The Crisis*, a magazine published by the National Association for the Advancement of Colored People.

Hunter, Richard — Unknown
Unfortunately, after much research, no bio information could be found on this poet.

Ish-Kishor, Judith – 1896–1977 – New York, USA
Ish-Kishor was born in England and is of Jewish heritage. She started writing poetry at age five and some of her poetry was published by age ten. At thirteen her family moved to New York City. She was published in multiple popular magazines. Her father was a popular author of children's literature for Jewish children.

Issac, Sophia — b. 2010 — Pensylavania, USA
Issac is Egyptian American, born in Cairo, Egypt and then her family moved to Pittsburgh, PA area with her parents and younger brothers when she was 3 years old. She loves to read and write and would love to be an author someday. She enjoys the poetry of Evaleen Stein and Henry Wadsworth Longfellow. "Mistress Winter" is her first published poem.

Larsen, Emilee — b. 2013 — Utah, USA
Larsen is thoughtful and imaginative. She loves reading, gymnastics, and Harry Potter. When Larsen grows up, she wants to be a librarian.

Larsen, Kiralee — b. 2010 — Utah, USA
Larsen was born in St. George, Utah. She loves to read, write, be artistic, learn, climb anything, and most importantly, enjoys the people in her life. Her poetry is highly influenced by her beloved family, her Father, Mother, and her five younger siblings (three sisters and two brothers). Her many friends are SUPER influential to her poetry as well. She loves writing poetry and has written over 35 poems. Larsen's poems "A Drop of Rain" and "Harry Potter's Glasses" were published in the 2023 publication of A Year of Poetry Tea Time Adventure.

Larsen, Lillee — b. 2014 — Utah, USA
Larsen is the third oldest of six. She loves to go on family vacations. She likes to climb trees, play with friends, and do gymnastics.

Larsen, Parker —b.2016 — Utah, USA
Larsen is imaginative, creative, and people enjoy being around his fun personality. He enjoys making forts, playing football, and drawing. He is the oldest boy in his family.

Lawrence D. H. —1885-1930 — England
Laurence was the fourth child of a miner who had little education and was illiterate. He had a rocky childhood and the turmoil of home provided a lot of the subject matter for his writing. His fist published book was The White Peacock in 1910.

Lincoln, Abraham — 1809-1865 — Kentucky, USA
Lincoln was the 16th President of the United States, serving from 1861 to 1865. Born in a log cabin in Kentucky, Lincoln largely self-educated himself and became a lawyer. He played a crucial role in preserving the Union during the American Civil War, and his leadership saw the issuance of the Emancipation Proclamation in 1863, which aimed to end slavery in Confederate-held territories. Lincoln's Gettysburg Address, delivered in 1863, is celebrated for its eloquence and its expression of dedication to the principles of equality and democracy. Tragically, he was assassinated by John Wilkes Booth in April 1865, just days after the end of the Civil War. Lincoln is widely revered as one of America's greatest presidents.

Longfellow, Henry Wadsworth — 1807-1882 — Massachusetts, USA

Longfellow was born in Portland, Maine and as a young child, he was bright and studious and learned Latin. In his lifetime he studied many languages. Longfellow attended Bowdoin College and later taught modern languages at Harvard University. His extensive travels in Europe and exposure to the works of European Romantic poets greatly influenced his writing. Longfellow's most famous works include "Paul Revere's Ride," "The Song of Hiawatha," and "Evangeline." These poems captured historical events, Native American legends, and themes of love and loss, and they earned him recognition and popularity in both the United States and Europe. His poetry, characterized by its musicality and storytelling, contributed to shaping American cultural identity during the 19th century, making him one of the most celebrated poets of his time. He was the first to translate *Dante's Divine Comedy*. In 1820 his first poem, "The Battle of Lovell's Pond," was published.

Ly You — 1125-1210 — China

Lu You (1125–1210) was a prominent Chinese poet of the Southern Song Dynasty. Known for his vast literary output, Lu You was a prolific writer of ci poetry, a distinctive form of lyric poetry. His works often expressed deep emotions, ranging from love and patriotism to reflections on life's impermanence. Despite facing personal hardships and political challenges, Lu You's poetry continued to resonate with later generations, making him one of the "Eight Immortals of the Ci School" and an influential figure in Chinese literary history.

Martin Luther — 1483-1546
Luther was a German monk, theologian, and key figure in the Protestant Reformation. He is best known for his Ninety-Five Theses, which he posted on the door of the Castle Church in Wittenberg in 1517, challenging certain practices of the Catholic Church. Luther's teachings emphasized salvation by faith alone, the authority of the Bible, and the priesthood of all believers, forming the basis of Protestantism. His actions and ideas had a profound impact on Christianity and led to significant religious and cultural changes in Europe.

Mathews, Henry — b. 2015 — Arizona, USA
Mathews is a young poet who has his publishing debut in this book. He penned the haiku "I Shiver So Cold."

Matsuo Basho – 1644–1694 – Japan
Matsuo Basho was born in Japan and introduced to poetry at a young age. He was the most famous poet during Japan's Edo period. He wrote in a special form of poetry named haiku (hokku). He was considered the master of haiku, but he felt that his true genius lay in another poetry form called renku.

Mitchell, Agnes E. — unknown — USA
The verse included in this book was a carved in wood adorning the Lizzie Borden's historical Maplecroft Mansion. William Ulrich did extensive research to discover who was the author of the verse. HE concluded that there was no answer to the mystery. Melissa Allen picket up the task years latter thinking that it was an exhausted search. After a long search and a lucky google search on a whim for "and old time friends and twilight plays" she found the poem it was extracted from. It was written by Agnes E. Mitchell for a publication called *Common-School Literature English and American with Several Hundred Extracts to be Memorized in 1876 with the simple title of "CCXLIV"*. You can see the entire poem titled "When the Cows Come Home" in the Bonus Poems section of this book.

Milne, A. A. — 1882-1956 — England
In 1903, Milne graduated from Cambridge with a mathematics degree. He served in both the First and Second World Wars. He wrote for *Punch* magazine and wrote eighteen plays and three books, one being *The Red House Mystery*. In 1924, two years after his son was born, he wrote a collection of poetry titled *When We Were Very Young*. His second collection of poetry, *Now We Are Six* was published in 1927. Milne's most enduring work, "Winnie-the-Pooh," and its sequel, "The House at Pooh Corner," introduced readers to the whimsical world of Christopher Robin and his friends in the Hundred Acre Wood. These stories have captured the hearts of generations and continue to be celebrated for their endearing characters and timeless themes of friendship and adventure.

Mother Goose — 17th Century — Unknown
Mother Goose is a fictional author's name given to a collection of rhymes and short stories. It is unknown where the name originated. People claim it originated in France, England, Germany, United States and more. The rhymes have been read to generations of children and we may never know who created them or when they were created.

McAboy, Mary R.T. — 1815-1892 — Kentucky, USA

McAboy was born and raised in Kentucky along with her four siblings. She was educated by her Uncle Hon. John Rootes Thornton who also raised her. He was a lawer and a Kentucky House of Representatives. For 30 years she wrote for many publications using the pen name M.R.M., Roseheath, KY." Roseheath was the name of the homestead she lived on. She had a collection of poems published in 1884 titled *Roseheath Poems*.

Owens, Christine — b. 1976 — California, USA

Born Christine Lynn Faulkner and raised in San Diego, California by Kenneth and Dennise (Prunty) Faulkner, Owens has enjoyed writing and drawing from a young age. She was married and traveled to twenty countries before having her four children. She draws inspiration from her life experiences and people she has met. She is the author of the books *Relaxed Homeschooling* and *A Year of Poetry Tea Time* and owner of A Year of Poetry Tea Time.

Peabody, Josephine Preston —1874-1922 — New York, USA

Peabody started to write poetry at a young age. She grew to love literature just like her parents. Peabody's first published work was a poem published in The Woman's Journal in 1888. Her first volume of verse, *The Wayfarers* (1898), was followed by *Fortune and Men's Eyes* (1900), a one-act play built on Shakespeare's sonnets, and *Marlowe* (1901), a verse play on Christopher Marlowe. From 1901 to 1903 she lectured on poetry and literature at Wellesley (Massachusetts) College.

Perrine, Niccole – b. 1983 – Idaho, USA
Perrine was born in Upstate New York, raised in Southern California and Southcentral Alaska. She made her home in Southwestern Idaho and is the mother of five and author of T*he Joy Series*.

Pierpont, James Lord — 1822-1893 — Massachusetts, USA
Pierpont was born in Boston, Massachusetts to a American songwriter and poet best known for composing the popular song "Jingle Bells." Born in Massachusetts to Reverend John Pierpont who was also a abolitionist and a poet. He attended a boarding school but at the age of ten he ran away and joined the crew of a whaling ship called the Shark. He then joined the US Navy till he was 21. Pierpont had a diverse career that included stints as a songwriter, organist, and even a performer in minstrel shows. "Jingle Bells," originally titled "The One Horse Open Sleigh," was written in 1857 and some historians mistakenly thought his father had written it. Despite his association with this festive classic, Pierpont's career encompassed various musical endeavors and contributions to the cultural landscape of his time.

Poe, Edgar Allen — 1809-1849 — Virginia, USA
Poe was born in Boston, Massachusetts, and then after his father left and mother died, he moved to Virginia with the Allen family. He attended WestPoint for a short time but when his foster mother, Frances Allan, passed away he no longer felt the need to impress John Allen and arranged to be released from the school. He spent most of his life with very little money. He released his first forty-page book of poetry at age eighteen titled, *Tamerlane and other Poems*. He was a poet, writer, editor, and a literary critic. He is most famous for his poem "The Raven" and he is said to be the originator of the detective story. His poetry is known for being dark and strange. And just like his poetry his death was never understood.

Revo, Sara —b. 2005 — Idaho, USA
Revo was born in Utah the 2nd child of tree. Years later, after she was married her family moved to Idaho. She has had poetry in her veins since she was young. Sometimes she writes her poetry based on a certain topic, or she'll have a rhythm come to mind and simply add words. She also loves history, especially studying the lives and words of many poets including Henry Wadsworth Longfellow, Edgar Guest, William Shakespeare, Hannah More, and more! Revo loves reading, writing, singing, sewing, and spending time with her amazing family.

Rossetti, Christina — 1830-1894 — England
Rossetti was of Italian descent and came from a family of writers and grew up to be a writer and poet herself. She was educated by her parents at home and was well versed in fairy tales, classics, and religious works. Her most famous collection of poems is titled *Goblin Market and Other Poems*. There are also two Christmas songs that are well known in England for which she wrote the text – "Love Came Down at Christmas" and "In the Bleak Midwinter."

Rullo, Luca — b.2011 — Connecticut, USA
Rullo is educated at home and enjoys the free time he has to devote to writing. He is born into a family with one other sibling, a brother. Rullo also enjoys his two guinea pigs. He loves sports, and playing the drums. He loves to think up ideas for stories, which comes from his love of reading.
He poem "My Protector" was published in the CT Bards Poetry Review in 2023.

Sabapathy, Mala — b. 2013 — Australia
Sabapathy enjoys writing both poetry and stories. With her poetry she is particularly inspired by nature, and loves capturing the beauty of the world in words. Aside from writing, Sabapathy loves drawing, dragons, animals and swimming. This is her second published poem. Her first poem, 'Sky Dragon,' was selected and published in the book *The Write Note* in 2021. Sabapathy began homeschooling in March 2023. She aspires to publish a book. In the future.

Salazar, Cristabella — b. 2011 — Virginia, USA
Salazar was born in Portsmouth, Virginia the youngest of five children. She has adopted her mother's love for poetry.

Salazar, Lee Ann — b. 1971 — Kentucky, USA
Salazar was born in Henderson, Kentucky the oldest of 4 children. Her interest in poetry was sparked in middle school. She entered a fiction writing competition called the Ohio River Arts Festival and had a poem published. She passed her love of poetry onto future students, 6 of who became published poets. She is now passing that same passion down to her own children.

Sandburg, Carl – 1878–1967 – Illinois, USA
Sandburg left school at the age of thirteen and did many different jobs. Later he became a journalist in Chicago. His time in Chicago would influence much of his writing. He won three Pulitzer Prizes, two for poetry collections and one for his biography of Abraham Lincoln. He is also famous for his *Rootabaga Stories* written for children.

Sangster, Margaret Elizabeth — 1838-1912 — New Jersey, USA
Sangster was born in New Rochelle, New York into a religious family. Her mother was from New York and her father was Irish. Her education happened primarily at home and showed an aptitude towards literature. she would write poems and short stories for prize money and would win often. She was published at age 17 with her children's book *Little Jamie*. She supported her family for 17 years through her journalistic work. She wrote for many different publications.

Schroeder, Elizabeth — b. 2006 — Colorado, USA
Schroeder has enjoyed writing poetry since she was about 10. But what really got her started was when she and her best friend decided to write gratitude poems and email them to each other during the Covid quarantine. It helped her stay positive and improved her writing. Schroeder had set a goal to be a published poet or author at age 17, and is proud to have achieved that goal!

Seaman, Hannah — b. 2008 — Zambia
Seaman was born in England but later her family moved to Zambia and grew up to love music. Song lyrics are like poems, so that inspired her to write her own. Her first published work is 'The Peak' in 2023. As a hobby, she also loves to make jewelry!

Seaman, Micah — b. 2013 — Zambia
Seaman was born in England and grew up to love Enid Blyton books. He draws inspiration for his poetry from his dreams and movies. In his spare time he enjoys playing Pokémon.

Shenkenberger, Amanda — b. 1988 — Oregon, USA
Shenkenberger is a former homeschooled kid turned homeschool mom turned homeschool coach. When her parents divorced, she found comfort and self-expression in poetry; the divorce also sent her to public high school. After a few months there, she declared, "This is stupid and I'm never sending my kids here," and she never has. Now she teaches other families how to create their family legacy through homeschooling. Adventuring through the Pacific Northwest with her high school sweetheart and their 4 boys, Amanda uses the time together to relish family and foster a deep love of learning.

Smith, Sandie — b. 1992 — Idaho, USA
Smith was born in Fairview, Idaho the sith child of eight siblings. She attended a class in high school and discovered that she very much enjoyed writing poetry. Smith currently lives in Idaho and enjoys drawing, writing, photography, playing guitar, and being active outdoors.

Somer, Alan — b. 1976 — Australia
Somer was born in Scotland and was in the Royal Navy for 17years. In 2013 he moved to Australia to marry his soulmate. He is now the National Program Manager for Buddy Up Australia, a Charity that runs social, physical and volunteer events for Veterans, First Responders and their families. Somer is attending a Veterans Bush Poetry workshop in Western Australia looking at the works of Banjo Paterson.

Somer, Alex — b. 2015 — Australia
Somer had his first poem published at the age of 8. He enjoys camping, gaming and his two cavoodle dogs Milo and Chip as well as spending time with friends.

Stevenson, Robert Louis — 1850-1894 — Scotland
Born in Edinburgh, Scotland, Stevenson had bronchial troubles his entire life which highly limited what he could do as a child. His nanny and mother would tell him stories to entertain him as a child. He dreamed of the grand adventures he would go on some day and let his imagination go wild. Stevenson initially studied law but soon pursued a career as a writer. He went on a Yacht adventure to the Pacific Islands to help his health. This trip gave him a lot of inspiration for his future writings. Not only is he known for his novels, *Treasure Island, Kidnapped, Strange Case of Dr. Jekyll and Mr. Hyde*, he is also very well known for his collection of children's poems titled *A Child's Garden of Verses*. Stevenson's writings often explored themes of duality, adventure, and the human condition, and his ability to captivate readers with suspenseful plots and c'mplex characters established him as a significant figure in English literature.

Sylvester, E. L. — ca. 1800's — USA
The poem "A Cup Of Tea" by E. L. Sylvester was published in the St. Nicholas Magazine in 1893. The magazine was a popular children's monthly publication who's first editor was poet Mary Mapes Dodge (poetry of hers also in this book). St. Nicholas Magazine published many famous poets to include Alcott, Burnett, Twain and more. The magazine was discontinued in 1840 and tried again in 1843 to only last a few issues.

Su Shi —1037-1101 — China
Su Shi (1037–1101), also known as Su Dongpo, was a prominent Chinese poet, scholar, and statesman during the Song Dynasty. His literary contributions extended to various genres, including poetry, prose, and calligraphy. Su Shi's poetry often conveyed a deep appreciation for nature, reflecting the Daoist and Confucian influences in his work. He is renowned for his wit, versatility, and his significant impact on the development of classical Chinese literature. Su Shi's enduring legacy encompasses not only his poetic achievements but also his contributions to calligraphy and governance during a transformative period in Chinese history.

Taylor, Korbin — b. 2011 — California, USA
Taylor was born and raised in California, the youngest of two children. There he lives with his family and loves to work on writing poetry and short stories with his sister Rhylin. He enjoys swimming on the local swim team and helping older community members keep up their gardens. He is an avid chess player and loves gardening and reading, especially science fiction

Taylor, Rhylin — b. 2009 — California, USA
Tylor was born in California and still resides there. She is the oldest of two children, her younger sibling being Korbin. Taylor also loves to act in her local community theater. She has always loved a variety of poetry from Dr. Seuss to Shakespeare. She has a passion for animals and has volunteered at the local cat shelter for the past 3 years. Taylor claims that "all of her literary success is due to his cats" Gladys, Leo and Flame Pelt.

Van Komen, Alex — b. 2006 — Ohio, USA
Van Komen is an enthusiast of reading and writing. If you find him without a book he would be playing piano or goofing off with his siblings. He hopes to someday be an author or teacher.

Van Komen, Spencer — b. 2010 — Ohio, USA
Van Komen has 56 animals that are under his care. He loves his dogs, bunny, cats, and ducks too much–and has too many chickens. When he's not taking care of his animals, Van Komen enjoys building trebuchets, catapults, and tinkering around with things.

Wang Asnshi, — 1021-1066 — China
Wang Anshi was a prominent Chinese poet, statesman, and reformer during the Song Dynasty. Known for his role in implementing social and economic reforms, Wang served as Chancellor of the Song government. Apart from his political activities, he was a prolific poet, and his literary contributions played a significant role in shaping the literary landscape of his time. Wang Anshi's poetry often reflected themes of nature, contemplation, and the human experience, showcasing his multifaceted talents as both a statesman and a literary figure in Chinese history.

Wen Zhengming — 1470-1559 — China
Wen Zhengming was a prominent Ming dynasty Chinese poet, painter, and calligrapher. Renowned for his accomplishments in both literature and the visual arts, Wen Zhengming was a leading figure in the Wu School of painting and a key proponent of literati painting. His poetry often explored themes of nature, friendship, and the contemplative life, showcasing a deep connection to traditional Chinese aesthetics. As a scholar-official, Wen Zhengming held various government positions, contributing to the cultural and artistic landscape of his time. His artistic legacy continues to influence Chinese ink painting and poetry.

Whitman, Walt — 1819 -1892 — New York, USA
Whitman was born in West Hills, New York. He came from a working-class family and had a limited formal education till the age of eleven. In 1855, he self-published a collection of poems titled "Leaves of Grass," a ground breaking work that defied traditional poetic conventions. "Leaves of Grass" is known for its free verse style and its celebration of the human spirit, nature, and the interconnectedness of all things. During the American Civil War, Whitman worked as a volunteer nurse, tending to wounded soldiers in Washington, D.C. His experiences during the war deeply influenced his poetry, leading to works like "Drum-Taps" and "Memories of President Lincoln." He is often regarded as one of the most influential American poets, and his works continue to be studied and celebrated for their artistic and philosophical significance. He combined the ideas of both transcendentalism and realism in his literature. He is well known for his poem "O Captain! My Captain!" (written after the death of Abraham Lincoln).

Williams, William Carlos — 1883-1963 — New Jersey, USA

Williams grew up in. a bilingual home speaking both English and Spanish. He earned both a Bachelor of Arts and a medical degree. He practiced pediatric and general medicine. Poetry was a passion of his and he did not stop writing poetry and was considered a key figure in the modernist poetry movement. His poetry used vivid imagery and shared his direct experience with the world around him. Some of Williams' most well-known works include "The Red Wheelbarrow," "This Is Just to Say," and the epic poem "Paterson." His collection "Spring and All" (1923) is regarded as a seminal work in American modernist poetry. In 1963, shortly after his death, he was posthumously awarded the Pulitzer Prize for Poetry for his collection "Pictures from Brueghel and Other Poems."

Wynne, Annette — before 1919 — USA

In 1919, her debut collection of children's poems, *For Days and Days: A year round treasury of child verse* was published. Three years later her collection *Treasure Things* was published in 1922. Her poetry was childlike and playful. This is what she said about her collection For Days and Days "The aim of these verses is to please children and others. They Were written, and arranged calendar-wise, for school children's entertainments. Most teachers and parents find a dearth of usable material for young people's recitations; it is a commonplace that all good poetry is not good for such purposes. An attempt has been made to furnish, for all sorts of days, material that is close to the children's experience and at the same time timely. This book, therefore, is offered in the hope that it will facilitate the search of parents and teachers for joyous relaxation in the Land of School and otherwheres"

BONUS POEMS

Noel: Christmas Eve 1913
By Robert Bridges

A frosty Christmas Eve
  when the stars were shining
Fared I forth alone
  where westward falls the hill,
And from many a village
  in the water'd valley
Distant music reach'd me
  peals of bells aringing:
The constellated sounds
  ran sprinkling on earth's floor
As the dark vault above
  with stars was spangled o'er.
Then sped my thoughts to keep
  that first Christmas of all
When the shepherds watching
  by their folds ere the dawn
Heard music in the fields
  and marveling could not tell
Whether it were angels
  or the bright stars singing.

Now blessed be the tow'rs
  that crown England so fair
That stand up strong in prayer
  unto God for our souls
Blessed be their founders
  (said I) an' our country folk
Who are ringing for Christ
  in the belfries to-night
With arms lifted to clutch
  the rattling ropes that race
Into the dark above
  and the mad romping din.

But to me heard afar
  it was starry music
Angels' song, comforting
  as the comfort of Christ
When he spake tenderly
  to his sorrowful flock:
The old words came to me
  by the riches of time
Mellow'd and transfigured
  as I stood on the hill
Heark'ning in the aspect
  of th' eternal silence.

On the Morning of Christ's Nativity
By John Milton

I

This is the month, and this the happy morn,
Wherein the Son of Heaven's eternal King,
Of wedded maid and Virgin Mother born,
Our great redemption from above did bring;
For so the holy sages once did sing,
  That he our deadly forfeit should release,
And with his Father work us a perpetual peace.

II

That glorious Form, that Light unsufferable,
And that far-beaming blaze of majesty,
Wherewith he wont at Heaven's high council-table
To sit the midst of Trinal Unity,
He laid aside, and, here with us to be,
  Forsook the Courts of everlasting Day,
And chose with us a darksome house of mortal clay.

III

Say, Heavenly Muse, shall not thy sacred vein
Afford a present to the Infant God?
Hast thou no verse, no hymn, or solemn strain,
To welcome him to this his new abode,
Now while the heaven, by the Sun's team untrod,
  Hath took no print of the approaching light,
And all the spangled host keep watch in squadrons bright?

IV

See how from far upon the Eastern road
The star-led Wisards haste with odours sweet!
Oh! run; prevent them with thy humble ode,
And lay it lowly at his blessèd feet;
Have thou the honour first thy Lord to greet,
  And join thy voice unto the Angel Quire,
From out his secret altar touched with hallowed fire.

The Hymn

I

  It was the winter wild,
    While the heaven-born child
  All meanly wrapt in the rude manger lies;
    Nature, in awe to him,
    Had doffed her gaudy trim,
  With her great Master so to sympathize:
It was no season then for her
To wanton with the Sun, her lusty Paramour.

II

  Only with speeches fair
    She woos the gentle air
  To hide her guilty front with innocent snow,
    And on her naked shame,
    Pollute with sinful blame,
  The saintly veil of maiden white to throw;
Confounded, that her Maker's eyes
Should look so near upon her foul deformities.

III

  But he, her fears to cease,
    Sent down the meek-eyed Peace:
  She, crowned with olive green, came softly sliding
    Down through the turning sphere,

    His ready Harbinger,
      With turtle wing the amorous clouds dividing;
And, waving wide her myrtle wand,
She strikes a universal peace through sea and land.

IV

    No war, or battail's sound,
      Was heard the world around;
  The idle spear and shield were high uphung;
    The hookèd chariot stood,
      Unstained with hostile blood;
  The trumpet spake not to the armèd throng;
And Kings sat still with awful eye,
As if they surely knew their sovran Lord was by.

V

    But peaceful was the night
      Wherein the Prince of Light
His reign of peace upon the earth began.
    The winds, with wonder whist,
      Smoothly the waters kissed,
  Whispering new joys to the mild Ocean,
Who now hath quite forgot to rave,
While birds of calm sit brooding on the charmed wave.

VI

    The stars, with deep amaze,
      Stand fixed in steadfast gaze,
  Bending one way their precious influence,
    And will not take their flight,
      For all the morning light,
  Or Lucifer that often warned them thence;
But in their glimmering orbs did glow,
Until their Lord himself bespake, and bid them go.

VII

  And, though the shady gloom
  Had given day her room,
 The Sun himself withheld his wonted speed,
  And hid his head of shame,
  As his inferior flame
 The new-enlightened world no more should need:
He saw a greater Sun appear
Than his bright Throne or burning axletree could bear.

VIII

  The Shepherds on the lawn,
  Or ere the point of dawn,
 Sat simply chatting in a rustic row;
  Full little thought they than
  That the mighty Pan
 Was kindly come to live with them below:
Perhaps their loves, or else their sheep,
Was all that did their silly thoughts so busy keep.

IX

  When such music sweet
  Their hearts and ears did greet
 As never was by mortal finger strook,
  Divinely-warbled voice
  Answering the stringèd noise,
 As all their souls in blissful rapture took:
The air, such pleasure loth to lose,
With thousand echoes still prolongs each heavenly close.

X

  Nature, that heard such sound
  Beneath the hollow round
 Of Cynthia's seat the airy Region thrilling,
  Now was almost won
  To think her part was done,
 And that her reign had here its last fulfilling:

She knew such harmony alone
Could hold all Heaven and Earth in happier union.

XI

    At last surrounds their sight
    A globe of circular light,
That with long beams the shamefaced Night arrayed;
    The helmèd Cherubim
    And sworded Seraphim
Are seen in glittering ranks with wings displayed,
Harping in loud and solemn quire,
With unexpressive notes, to Heaven's newborn Heir.

XII

    Such music (as 'tis said)
    Before was never made,
But when of old the Sons of Morning sung,
    While the Creator great
    His constellations set,
And the well-balanced World on hinges hung,
And cast the dark foundations deep,
And bid the weltering waves their oozy channel keep.

XIII

    Ring out, ye crystal spheres!
    Once bless our human ears,
If ye have power to touch our senses so;
    And let your silver chime
    Move in melodious time;
And let the bass of heaven's deep organ blow;
And with your ninefold harmony
Make up full consort of the angelic symphony.

XIV

    For, if such holy song
    Enwrap our fancy long,
  Time will run back and fetch the Age of Gold;
    And speckled Vanity
    Will sicken soon and die,
  And leprous Sin will melt from earthly mould;
And Hell itself will pass away,
And leave her dolorous mansions of the peering day.

XV

    Yes, Truth and Justice then
    Will down return to men,
  The enamelled arras of the rainbow wearing;
    And Mercy set between,
    Throned in celestial sheen,
  With radiant feet the tissued clouds down steering;
And Heaven, as at some festival,
Will open wide the gates of her high palace-hall.

XVI

    But wisest Fate says No,
    This must not yet be so;
  The Babe lies yet in smiling infancy
    That on the bitter cross
    Must redeem our loss,
  So both himself and us to glorify:
Yet first, to those chained in sleep,
The wakeful trump of doom must thunder through the deep,

XVII

    With such a horrid clang
    As on Mount Sinai rang,
  While the red fire and smouldering clouds outbrake:
    The aged Earth, aghast
    With terror of that blast,
Shall from the surface to the centre shake,

When, at the world's last sessiön,
The dreadful Judge in middle air shall spread his throne.

XVIII

   And then at last our bliss
   Full and perfect is,
But now begins; for from this happy day
   The Old Dragon under ground,
   In straiter limits bound,
Not half so far casts his usurpèd sway,
And, wroth to see his Kingdom fail,
Swindges the scaly horror of his folded tail.

XIX

   The Oracles are dumb;
   No voice or hideous hum
Runs through the archèd roof in words deceiving.
   Apollo from his shrine
   Can no more divine,
Will hollow shriek the steep of Delphos leaving.
No nightly trance, or breathèd spell,
Inspires the pale-eyed Priest from the prophetic cell.

XX

   The lonely mountains o'er,
   And the resounding shore,
A voice of weeping heard and loud lament;
   Edgèd with poplar pale,
   From haunted spring, and dale
The parting Genius is with sighing sent;
With flower-inwoven tresses torn
The Nymphs in twilight shade of tangled thickets mourn.

XXI

   In consecrated earth,
   And on the holy hearth,
The Lars and Lemures moan with midnight plaint;

    In urns, and altars round,
    A drear and dying sound
  Affrights the Flamens at their service quaint;
And the chill marble seems to sweat,
While each peculiar power forgoes his wonted seat.

XXII

    Peor and Baälim
    Forsake their temples dim,
  With that twice-battered god of Palestine;
    And moonèd Ashtaroth,
    Heaven's Queen and Mother both,
  Now sits not girt with tapers' holy shine:
The Libyc Hammon shrinks his horn;
In vain the Tyrian maids their wounded Thammuz mourn.

XXIII

    And sullen Moloch, fled,
    Hath left in shadows dread
  His burning idol all of blackest hue;
    In vain with cymbals' ring
    They call the grisly king,
  In dismal dance about the furnace blue;
The brutish gods of Nile as fast,
Isis, and Orus, and the dog Anubis, haste.

XXIV

    Nor is Osiris seen
    In Memphian grove or green,
  Trampling the unshowered grass with lowings loud;
    Nor can he be at rest
    Within his sacred chest;
  Nought but profoundest Hell can be his shroud;
In vain, with timbreled anthems dark,
The sable-stolèd Sorcerers bear his worshiped ark.

XXV

    He feels from Juda's land
      The dreaded Infant's hand;
  The rays of Bethlehem blind his dusky eyn;
    Nor all the gods beside
      Longer dare abide,
  Not Typhon huge ending in snaky twine:
Our Babe, to show his Godhead true,
Can in his swaddling bands control the damnèd crew.

XXVI

    So, when the Sun in bed,
      Curtained with cloudy red,
  Pillows his chin upon an orient wave,
    The flocking shadows pale
      Troop to the infernal jail,
  Each fettered ghost slips to his several grave,
And the yellow-skirted Fays
Fly after the night-steeds, leaving their moon-loved maze.

XXVII

    But see! the Virgin blest
      Hath laid her Babe to rest,
  Time is our tedious song should here have ending:
    Heaven's youngest-teemèd star
      Hath fixed her polished car,
  Her sleeping Lord with handmaid lamp attending;
And all about the courtly stable
Bright-harnessed Angels sit in order serviceable.

AVAILABLE ON AMAZON
Learn more at
AYearofPoetryTeaTime.com

2024 THE International Homeschooling POETRY CONTEST SPRING

A Year of Poetry Tea Time is sponsoring the 4th International Homeschooling Poetry contest to give Homeschoolers all over the world a chance to be published.
Contest is open to both children and adults of **Homeschooling families.**

20+ poets will be published - This years theme is Sping
Four separate age groups - Contest begins April 1st, 2024

Enter up to 3 Poems

Contest Begins

Up To **$1200** in Prizes

Deadline

To learn more about the Theme, Prizes, and Rules Visit
www.ayearofpoetryteatime/poetrycontest
email: ayearofpoetryteatime@gmail.com

Made in United States
Troutdale, OR
12/18/2023

16191306R00120